Items should be returned on or before the last date
shown below. Items not already requested by other
borrowers may be renewed in person, in writing or by
telephone. To renew, please quote the number on the
barcode label. To renew online a PIN is required.
This can be requested at your local library.
Renew online @ **www.dublincitypubliclibraries.ie**
Fines charged for overdue items will include postage
incurred in recovery. Damage to or loss of items will
be charged to the borrower.

Leabharlanna Poiblí Chathair Bhaile Átha Cliath
Dublin City Public Libraries

Baile Átha Cliath
Dublin City

Date Due	Date Due	Date Due
14/2		
2 6 NOV 2018		

Maynooth Studies in Irish Local History

SERIES EDITOR   Raymond Gillespie

This is one of six new pamphlets in the Maynooth Studies in Irish Local History Series to be published in the year 2000. Like their predecessors, most of the pamphlets are based on theses completed as part of the M.A. in local history programme in National University of Ireland, Maynooth. While the regions and time span which they cover are diverse, from Waterford to Monaghan, and from the fourteenth to the twentieth centuries, they all share a conviction that the exploration of the local past can shed light on the evolution of modern societies. They each demonstrate that understanding the evolution of local societies is important. The local worlds of Ireland in the past are as complex and sophisticated as the national framework in which they are set. The communities which peopled those local worlds, whether they be the inhabitants of religious houses, industrial villages or rural parishes, shaped and were shaped by their environments to create a series of interlocking worlds of considerable complexity. Those past worlds are best interpreted not through local administrative divisions, such as the county, but in human units: local places where communities of people lived and died. Untangling what held these communities together, and what drove them apart, gives us new insights into the world we have lost.

These pamphlets each make a significant contribution to understanding Irish society in the past. Together with twenty-eight earlier works in this series they explore something of the hopes and fears of those who lived in Irish local communities in the past. In doing so they provide examples of the practice of local history at its best and show the vibrant discipline which the study of local history in Ireland has become in recent years.

Maynooth Studies in Irish Local History: Number 29

Canon Frederick Donovan's Dunlavin 1884–1896

A west Wicklow village in the late nineteenth century

Chris Lawlor

IRISH ACADEMIC PRESS

DUBLIN • PORTLAND, OR

First published in 2000 by
IRISH ACADEMIC PRESS
44, Northumberland Road, Dublin 4, Ireland
and in the United States of America by
IRISH ACADEMIC PRESS
c/o ISBS, 5804 NE Hassalo Street, Portland, OR 97213–3644.

website: www.iap.ie

© Chris Lawlor 2000

British Library Cataloguing in Publication Data
Lawlor, Chris, 1960–
    Canon Frederick Donovan's Dunlavin, 1884–1896 : a west Wicklow village in the
    late nineteenth century. – (Maynooth studies in Irish local history; no. 29)
    1. Donovan, Frederick Augustine   2. Catholic Church – Ireland   3. Dunlavin
    (Ireland)   – History – 19th century
    I. Title
    941.8'4'09034
    ISBN 0–7165–2724–3

Library of Congress Cataloging-in-Publication Data
Lawlor, Chris, 1960–
    Canon Frederick Donovan's Dunlavin, 1884–1896 : a west Wicklow village in
    the late nineteenth century / Chris Lawlor.
        p.   cm. — (Maynooth studies in local history ; no. 29)
    Partly based on a diary by Frederick Augustine Donovan.
        ISBN 0–7165–2724–3 (pbk)
        1. Dunlavin (Ireland)—History. 2. Donovan, Frederick Augustine—Diaries.
    3. Villages—Ireland—Wicklow—History—19th century.   4. Catholic Church—
    Ireland—Dunlavin—Clergy—Diaries. 5. Canons, cathedral, collegiate, etc.—
    Ireland—Diaries.   I. Donovan, Frederick Augustine.   II. Title.   III. Series.

    DA995D972 L38 2000
    941.8'4—dc21   00–044839

Typeset in 10 pt on 12 pt Bembo by
Carrigboy Typesetting Services, County Cork
Printed by ColourBooks Ltd., Dublin

Contents

Preface

I wish to thank a number of people who helped me with this pamphlet: Prof. Vincent Comerford, Dr. Raymond Gillespie, Rev. Patrick Finn, Rev. Michael Murphy, Rev. Bill Bowder, George Coleborn, my M.A. classmates, and the extremely helpful staffs of all the repositories: National Library, National Archives, Dublin Diocesan Archive, R.C.B. Library, Russell and John Paul II Libraries (Maynooth), Trinity College Library, Kildare and Wicklow County Libraries, Naas Library and Dunlavin library. Particularly I should like to thank my wife, Margaret, and my sons, Declan, Jason and Michael, for all their help and support.

Introduction

This pamphlet examines the west Wicklow village of Dunlavin and its rural hinterland during the last two decades of the nineteenth century. It attempts to reconstruct, partially at least, the community and conditions within the area at that time. The central figure is Canon Frederick Augustine Donovan P.P., V.F., who was parish priest of Dunlavin from 1884 to 1896. Donovan kept a diary during his time in Dunlavin, and this valuable manuscript source survives in the sacristy of Dunlavin Roman Catholic church. Hopefully this pamphlet will make Donovan's diary more widely known.

No study of Dunlavin in the late nineteenth century has been published except Rev. Samuel Russell McGee's booklet *Dunlavin – a retrospect 1894–1905* (Dublin, 1935). McGee's work is mainly anecdotal and is centred within the land-owning upper class of the Dunlavin region. McGee was the Church of Ireland rector of Dunlavin from 1894 to 1905 and his work contains few references to the Catholic parish, although the area was demographically dominated by Roman Catholics in the late nineteenth century. Catholic dominated movements such as the National League and the National Federation have not been studied in the Dunlavin area. James Whittle's *Sons of Saint Nicholas – a history of Dunlavin G.A.A. club* (Dunlavin, 1984) contains some references to Dunlavin in the late nineteenth century, but these are understandably brief as the club was only formed in 1890.

This study is different. It attempts to take a broader view of the area during the 1880s and 1890s than the work of either McGee or Whittle. The present work attempts to recreate late nineteenth-century Dunlavin as Canon Donovan perceived it. It is not a biography of Donovan, nor is it an account of the devotional revolution in Dunlavin. Equally it is not a history of local politics in the village at the time. The school of 'new history' now delves into the history of ordinary people as they saw it themselves – an idea put very well by Prof. P. J. Corish when he speaks of 'the often secret life of the small folk who live among small things.'[1] Donovan fits this description. He was not a nationally known figure. He did not make the hierarchy. He was parish priest of a small west Wicklow village. In the big picture, he was not 'important' – but to his parishioners in Dunlavin at the time, Donovan was a very significant figure and his diary provides a unique window into what would have been otherwise a 'secret life'.

Donovan's diary is the principal source from which this study is drawn and I make no apology for using one source so heavily. The diary contains records of the things which Donovan perceived to be important. It is in the spirit of the local historian looking at the history of a nineteenth-century parish priest as he saw it himself that Donovan's diary is utilised. As sources, diaries have some drawbacks. W. G. Hoskins, the great English local historian, stated that 'the deficiencies of [a diary] from the historical point of view will be obvious enough . . . the diarist is likely to be giving a highly subjective impression of an event or a person and such a record should be treated with proper caution'. However Hoskins goes on to say that diaries 'represent a record made at the time and, being unofficial, probably reflect more of the truth than an official and edited version is likely to do'.[2] Donovan's diary is an important historical source for Dunlavin and it is much more likely to give us an insight into Canon Donovan's Dunlavin than any printed parliamentary paper, newspaper article or nineteenth-century directory could ever do. Diaries may have drawbacks as sources, but, as long as the reader realises this, they are an excellent source to use, as the work of Dermot James and Séamas Ó Maitiú on the diaries of Elizabeth Smith demonstrates for the west Wicklow area.[3]

The pamphlet also draws on other sources besides Donovan's diary. These include printed sources such as *Slater's* and *Thom's* directories. Though concise, the amount of information that they contain is limited. Parliamentary papers, for instance the *Agricultural Statistics for Ireland*, provide in-depth information about certain aspects of life in the Dunlavin region at the time, but they may not be totally accurate. This is also true for data taken from the censuses. Manuscript sources used include the Shearman papers, a cornucopia of information about the Dunlavin area, housed in the Russell Library, N.U.I. Maynooth. However Shearman, who was curate of Dunlavin from 1862 to 1867, was writing twenty years before Donovan, so the collection is only useful as background information to Donovan's Dunlavin. Some small fragments were found among the Walsh papers in the Dublin Diocesan Archive, but Donovan does not seem to have corresponded with Archbishop Walsh. He did correspond with the press. The *Leinster Leader* was a particularly useful source but strongly biased towards the nationalists' viewpoint, as it was a rival to the Unionist *Kildare Observer*. Taken together, these and other sources, including some secondary sources such as the works by Russell McGee and Whittle provide a backdrop and flesh out the material that Donovan's diary contains about his Dunlavin world.

This pamphlet looks into Donovan's Dunlavin world and is divided into three parts. The first chapter sets the scene. The location of Dunlavin parish and its topographical divisions are noted. The means of livelihood of the people living in the area are examined, both in the rural hinterland and in Dunlavin village itself. The economic situation within the region at the time is studied in conjunction with its demography. Divisions within the population, in terms of religion, wealth, landholding and politics are examined. These become more important and more evident in later chapters. The second chapter examines ecclesiastical life and religiosity in Dunlavin during the late nineteenth century. The experience of the Catholic parish of Dunlavin is seen through Donovan's eyes. Thus improvements to the churches, schools and parochial houses, which were important to Donovan himself, were recorded. Such improvements made Donovan a significant agent of the devotional revolution in Dunlavin, but Donovan would be surprised to learn this, as the term 'devotional revolution' is a twentieth-century one.[4] The devotional experience of the Catholic parish as recorded by Donovan is examined and juxtaposed with the type of religiosity experienced at the local holy well. A brief study of the Protestant parish of Dunlavin, based mainly on McGee's *Retrospect*, is also included for the purposes of comparison and contrast. A sectarian element sometimes crept into local politics in the region, which are examined in the third chapter. Donovan was strongly nationalist and deeply involved in the Land League's successor, the Irish National League. After the Parnell split in 1891 Donovan was a leading figure in the anti-Parnellite Irish National Federation in Dunlavin. A rising tide of nationalism is revealed in the third chapter but this is tempered by internal feuds and divisions in which Donovan was a central figure. For this reason the priest's diary is an invaluable source for local politics in the Dunlavin region during the 1880s and 1890s, sometimes as important for what it does not record as much as for what Donovan actually wrote about. The third chapter sees developments in the political sphere through the eyes of Donovan himself.

To sum up, this pamphlet aims to bring to light an untapped primary source, dealing with an untapped area of study, religion and politics in late nineteenth-century Dunlavin. Dunlaviners at that time fitted the description of villagers given by Raymond Gillespie and Gerard Moran: 'part of a wider economic community through the network of markets and fairs in which they sold their surplus produce; part of the larger ecclesiastical community through the structures of their church and part of a larger political and legal structure through the presence of . . . government in the localities'.[5] Canon Donovan's diary makes it possible to turn the microscope on one village community, and as H.P.R. Finberg stated 'The microscope also has its uses. Within the nation there are smaller communities which have every right to be considered as distinct articulations of the national life'.[6] Canon Donovan lived in one such community.

Donovan's place: the Dunlavin
region 1881–1901

Dunlavin village is situated in west Wicklow, close to the border with County Kildare. In 1881 the settlement contained the mother church of both Roman Catholic and Church of Ireland parishes and acted as a nodal market town for the surrounding hinterland. This chapter constructs a picture of the Dunlavin area and its community as it was during the tenure of Fr. Frederick Augustine Donovan as parish priest. Donovan presided over the Catholic parish of Dunlavin from 1884 to 1896, but the period covered by this study has been slightly extended to encompass the years from 1881 to 1901 in order to utilise source material from the censuses of those years.

Some years later, in 1926, Dunlavin's parish priest Fr. Patrick O'Byrne gave an accurate description of his domain when he wrote: 'Geographically the parish of Dunlavin, entirely within west Wicklow, touches upon Hollywood, Ballymore-Eustace, Kilcullen and Narraghmore and forms to a great extent and for many miles the north-western boundary for Co. Wicklow. We run along the frontier from Tober to Colbinstown station'.[1] This is a very accurate description but it does not provide the full picture of the area. Dunlavin parish lies mainly in the barony of Lower Talbotstown (apart from the townland of Ballylea, which is in Upper Talbotstown). Lower Talbotstown is a very mountainous area and 39 per cent of the barony was classified as unproductive land in 1880.[2] Much of the barony lies over the 1,000 foot contour line, and Dunlavin parish itself extends almost to the summit of Lugnaquilla, 3,017 feet in altitude. In fact the parish may be quite neatly divided into two halves, upland and lowland. The upland part of the parish, with the village of Donard acting as a lower order services centre, comprises the Donard-Davidstown-Glen of Imaal region. People in this upland region had only limited contact with Dunlavin village itself. Samuel Russell McGee, rector of Dunlavin from 1894 to 1905, once asked a resident of Dunlavin village about some local people who were approaching, only to be told 'They're mountainy men, they're not like us'.[3] Another example of the psychological division within the parish was Fr. Donovan's decision not to speak at the Donard meeting at the time of the Orange outrage on Donard church in 1888 (see the third chapter). Donovan was content to leave the issue to his Donard curate, Fr. Brennan, as he perceived the upland Donard-centred area to be a distinct geographical unit. The psychological division of the parish into two regions mirrored the

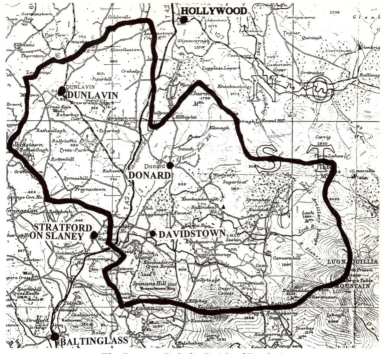

1. The Roman Catholic Parish of Dunlavin

physical reality. Soils in the Donard-centred upland region were acidic and there were many outcrops of granite on the steep slopes. This upland region was unsuitable for most types of agriculture, with the exception of sheep farming, which was an important activity. In 1880 there were 32,423 sheep recorded for the barony of Lower Talbotstown, while neighbouring Upper Talbotstown only recorded 18,413 sheep for that year.[4] Sheep were numerous – and vital – in Lower Talbotstown. Another indication of the poor quality of the land in the mountainous barony of Lower Talbotstown was the valuation figure for the barony. In 1874, the valuation of Lower Talbotstown, which covered 86,858 acres, was £28,080, while neighbouring Upper Talbotstown was valued at £32,398, despite consisting of only 62,310 acres.[5] Within the parish of Dunlavin, valuation figures also provided a contrast between the upland and lowland portions. Using Griffith's *Valuation* of 1854 and comparing townlands of similar size in the upland and lowland parts of Dunlavin parish gives us a stark, if not unexpected, contrast. Irishtown Park (upland, 95 acres) was valued at £48 5s. while Brewershill (lowland, 88 acres) was £60 10s.; Donard Lower (upland, 187 acres) was £92 12s. while Forristeen (lowland, 197 acres) was £140 5s.[6] Many other instances occur in Griffith's *Valuation*, but these two examples provide evidence of the division of wealth in Dunlavin parish, with the upland area centred on Donard lagging behind economically.

Below Donard and its mountains, nestling in the foothills, lies the other lowland half of Dunlavin parish, centred on the village of Dunlavin itself. The village dates from the late seventeenth century, and owes its origin to the Bulkeley family.[7] The motive for the foundation of the village was noted by the traveller Thomas Molyneaux in 1709 when he wrote: 'Dunlavin, a dirty village but prettily situated on a hill belonging to Sir Richard Buckley [sic.] who thought of establishing a university and building a colledge here; nay, went so far as to have bricks burnt for this purpose, but I think that project is now at an end.'[8] In 1702 Hesther Bulkeley, who had inherited the estate, married James Worth-Tynte, thus beginning the long association of the Tynte family with Dunlavin and ending the Bulkeley era.[9] While it did not become the university town envisaged by Sir Richard Bulkeley, the village of Dunlavin grew quickly during the eighteenth century. It became a planned landlord village with wide streets, a market square and a fairly uniform roof line – all typical Georgian village features. The most obvious sign of the improving spirit in eighteenth-century Dunlavin was the building of a fine market house. This was erected in 1737 by Robert Tynte at a cost of £2,000, of which £1,700 was advanced by Tynte's cousin Bulkeley.[10] The village continued to grow into the nineteenth century despite the violent events in the area during the period 1798 to 1803.[11] The 1821 census, the first real census of Ireland (however unreliable it might have been)[12] showed that the village of Dunlavin had a population of 897 people, while the surrounding area supported even more people – 1,495 according to the census.[13] In 1821 the village was on the main road to Tullow and Wexford, but in 1829 a new section of road was built bypassing Dunlavin.[14] Despite the loss of its main road status, the population of the village continued to expand and by the 1840s the population had almost reached the 1,000 mark. A relief commission letter, dated 17 January 1847 refers to 'Dunlavin, population 990 [a figure taken from the 1841 census], a comparatively good market town, the capital of a great district . . . it is chiefly supplied from Naas.'[15] As well as indicating population growth, this letter suggests that Dunlavin had links to County Kildare as well as to west Wicklow. As the village lies only one mile from the Kildare border, this was hardly surprising.

The Famine had a devastating effect on Dunlavin and its hinterland. As well as immediate loss of life and emigration – a comparison of the 1841 and 1851 population figures shows that the population of the village dropped from 990 to 757 while the surrounding area figure decreased even more dramatically from 1,604 to 984[16] – the Famine had long term effects on the population structure of the area. Censuses were taken in 1881, 1891 and 1901 and I have constructed population pyramids for Dunlavin District Electoral Division (D.E.D.) using the census data.

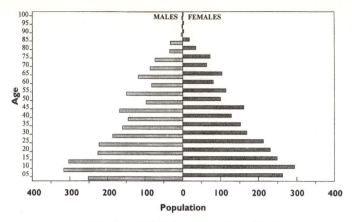

2. Dunlavin D.E.D. Population Pyramid 1881

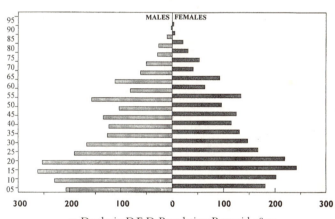

3. Dunlavin D.E.D. Population Pyramid 1891

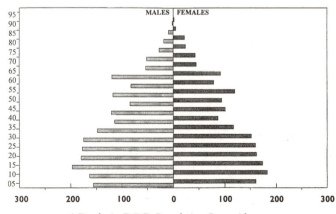

4. Dunlavin D.E.D. Population Pyramid 1901

Though a useful aid to the local historian, population pyramids are not without their problems. Firstly, the three pyramids only pertain to the three census years. Each pyramid represents a snapshot of Dunlavin D.E.D.'s population at a particular time. Each pyramid represents a synchronic situation and using them to build a diachronic picture could be misleading. For example, compensating falls and rises within age-heapings which occurred in mid-decade would not show up. However, the pyramids can certainly hint at trends during the twenty-year study period. Secondly, despite the best efforts of the authorities, no census is ever totally accurate. Even in the very comprehensive census of 1901, the number of females at school in Dunlavin is given as ninety and ninety-one in two different tables.[17] Thirdly, the use of five-year age heaping in population pyramids does not permit us to construct a detailed picture of the population. An economic boom followed suddenly by a crash and economic slump, for example, could reduce the birth rate very quickly. If this were so, the number of four-year-olds could be a lot larger than the number of one-year-olds in the 0–5 age heaping but we cannot see this from the population pyramid.

Nonetheless, population pyramids do reveal a significant amount of information. The 1881 population pyramid shows that the total population of the D.E.D. was 5,114. This was made up of 2,661 males and 2,453 females. The surplus of males over females remains a feature of all three population pyramids, indicating either a difference of migrational patterns between the sexes, or poorer female health and health care (or a combination of such factors). The effect of the Famine is still evident in the 1881 pyramid and some age groups are unnaturally small. The first of these is the 35–40 age group. Thirty-five years before 1881, the year was 1846. No doubt the Famine decimated birth rates nation-wide, but this population pyramid provides evidence of how the national catastrophe impacted at local level in Dunlavin D.E.D. The Roman Catholic baptismal registers in Dunlavin parish provide further evidence of the falling birth rate in Dunlavin during the Famine. For example the period between 1816 and 1821 saw 1,386 baptisms recorded, but the years from 1846 to 1851 only had 795 baptisms. This represents a 43 per cent drop on the earlier period. Even within the 1846–1851 period, the trend is constantly diminishing. The year 1846 saw 196 baptisms, while 1851 saw only 95 – a 53 per cent decrease.[18] Indeed, the numbers in the 30–35 age heaping on the pyramid are not much bigger indicating that the low birth rate continued through the Famine years up to 1851. Another small distortion on the 1881 pyramid occurs in the 45–50 group. Again, this could be a throwback to the Famine, as these people would have been children or young teenagers when the Famine struck. The young were particularly susceptible to death from disease or starvation, and many children emigrated with their families. Thus death and emigration are possible causes of the small numbers in this age grouping. The 55–60 age group is also very small. These people would have been in their early twenties during the Famine, and many Famine emigrants were in this age bracket when they left the country. Young couples especially tended to emigrate.[19] Perhaps the ties to land and native place were not as strong in this group as they were in older couples during the Famine years. The age groups above sixty-five years show a constantly diminishing trend as one moves upwards in age, but it is difficult to draw conclusions about the effects of the great Famine on these older strata of the population of Dunlavin D.E.D. as ageing would naturally account for such a diminishing trend.

It is youth not age that dominates the 1881 pyramid however, as 42 per cent of the total population was twenty years of age or less. This meant that the non-productive sector of the population (under 15s and over 65s) accounted for 41 per cent of the total. This is a high dependency ratio and would have put a considerable economic strain on the community. Dunlavin was in Baltinglass poor law union, and the master and matron of Baltinglass workhouse, Thomas and Susan Allen, had a number of inmates from the Dunlavin area.[20] The high proportion of children in Dunlavin D.E.D. in 1881 meant that John Lynch of Baltinglass, who had the medical contract for Dunlavin district, was kept busy attending to childhood ailments.[21] Another feature associated with such a youthful population was continued emigration. The population pyramid shows a large decline in the number of males between the 10–15 and 15–20 age groups. Almost all children had left school by the age of fifteen,[22] so the 25 per cent drop between these male age groupings indicates that many male teenagers left the area in search of work. The largest percentage decline in the population of young females on the other hand occurred between the 5–10 and the 10–15 age groups. This 15 per cent decrease shows that females left the area to take up employment, in positions such as shop assistants or domestic servants for example, at a younger age than male workers. In fact, there was an exodus of teenagers of both sexes from Dunlavin D.E.D. around this time, but this is not the most striking feature of the 1881 population pyramid. This distinction surely applies to the sudden, sharp and very recent decline in the birth rate. This drop is accentuated by the fact that the 5–10 year age grouping is the largest single group of both males and females in the whole 1881 pyramid. The drop in birth rate obviously occurred in the late 1870s, which were bad years economically. 'The fall in agricultural prices, which had begun about 1876, had been accompanied by several bad harvests, which destroyed millions of pounds worth of crops. In the west, where the potato was badly damaged, many small holders faced famine'.[23]

The threat of famine at this time applied as much to west Wicklow as to the west of Ireland. Dunlavin's mountainous Wicklow hinterland had more in common with the west of Ireland than it did with lowland Leinster, and the

threat of famine was very real in the area, which was a probable factor in the
15.6 per cent drop in the birth rate shown in the 1881 population pyramid.
The agricultural depression was real enough too. If the year 1875 is used as a
base of 100 for national agricultural prices, by 1880 practically every category
in the table showed a drop in price. Wheat, barley, potatoes, butter, eggs and
beef were all below the 1875 prices, while mutton was unchanged. The sole
category to record an increase in price was store cattle and that was not a large
increase for a five year period.[24] Although prices from Dunlavin fairs and
markets were not published in the local papers, the principal one of which,
the *Leinster Leader*, only dates from October 1880, the agricultural statistics for
Ireland reveal that the effects of the national agricultural depression were
hitting the Dunlavin area at this time also. Tables 1 and 2 show land use and
livestock numbers in Lower Talbotstown barony during the period 1875–1880.
Land under crops had increased slightly from 14,196 acres in 1875 to 14,713
acres in 1880, but land under grass had decreased significantly from 46,641
acres to 37,095. The real indicator of depression though was the increase of

Table 1 Land use by acreage in the barony of Lower Talbotstown 1875–1880

Year	Crops	Grass	Fallow	Woods	Waste
1875	14,196	46,641	2	895	25,124
1876	14,746	42,506	5	1,679	27,922
1877	14,237	36,698	6	1,302	34,615
1878	13,872	39,060	10	1,506	32,410
1879	13,893	43,940	9	1,784	27,232
1880	14,713	37,095	31	1,875	33,644

Source: *Agricultural statistics*

Table 2 Livestock numbers in the barony of Lower Talbotstown 1875–1880

Year	Horses	Cattle	Sheep	Pigs	Goats	Poultry	Asses
1875	1,407	13,862	28,513	3,045	571	25,472	432
1876	1,326	14,094	30,331	3,458	623	29,221	445
1877	1,547	13,033	24,598	3,683	632	28,636	473
1878	1,760	13,909	28,490	3,502	619	28,607	408
1879	1,640	14,235	41,400	2,775	571	27,265	455
1880	1,622	13,454	32,423	2,101	699	30,586	487

Source: *Agricultural statistics*

waste land (mainly mountain, bog and water) from 25,124 acres in 1875 to 33,644 acres in 1880.[25] Coupled with the fall in agricultural prices, this decrease in agricultural production hit farmers in the Dunlavin area very hard. More detail can be gleaned by examining the agricultural statistics from Dunlavin's poor law union (Baltinglass). Production of oats, the main cereal, was down from a very substantial 133,192 cwts. in 1875 to 118,870 cwts. in 1880. Potato production had dropped from 14,923 tons to 12,215 tons in the same period and hay was down from 38,893 tons to 34,185 tons. This latter fact was hardly surprising, as livestock figures in the poor law union had decreased too. Cattle were down from 31,980 in 1875 to 29,512 in 1880 while sheep numbers (important in such a mountainous area) had dropped from 44,560 in 1875 to 42,889 in 1880. Pigs too had decreased in numbers during this period, from 8,520 to 5,737. Money was scarce, and sidelines to farming such as pig-keeping obviously suffered heavily. Even the number of goats (again a feature of mountainous areas) had decreased, from 1,638 in 1875 to 1,552 in 1880.

The years after 1880 saw a gradual improvement in the fortunes of farmers in the area, however, and 27 per cent of the land in Baltinglass poor law union was under crops by 1886, up from 25 per cent in 1881. The numbers of livestock were also increasing and in 1886 there were 29,844 cattle in the poor law union (up from 28,348 in 1881). Sheep numbers had declined from 43,190 in 1881 to 39,677 in 1886, but the number of pigs was up from 7,500 in 1881 to 8,352 in 1886. Farmers once again had some ready money to finance pig keeping as a peripheral agricultural activity. The number of goats in the poor law union had risen from 9,950 in 1881 to 10,950 in 1886 and even the numbers of poultry (another peripheral farming occupation) had risen from 71,702 to 73,022 during this period.[26]

The evidence suggests that the agricultural depression hit the Dunlavin area badly during the late 1870s, but that the situation improved in the years after 1880. Further indications that this was indeed the case may be found by studying the numbers of buildings in Dunlavin district electoral division during the period from 1881 to 1901. Such data is a good economic indicator as large numbers of houses being built would indicate economic prosperity, while large numbers of uninhabited houses would show economic decline and emigration. However, other factors must also be taken into consideration. The number of houses being built in Dunlavin would have been dependent on landlord policy as well as the actual numbers of people in the area, while uninhabited houses could be quickly tumbled to clear land for agriculture, which was staging a recovery after 1881. Figure 5 shows the number of buildings in Dunlavin D.E.D. during the census years of 1881, 1891 and 1901 and figure 6 shows the number of buildings in Dunlavin village in those years. Both figures are similar, showing a decline in the number of houses and, perhaps more significantly, a decline in the number of inhabited houses. The

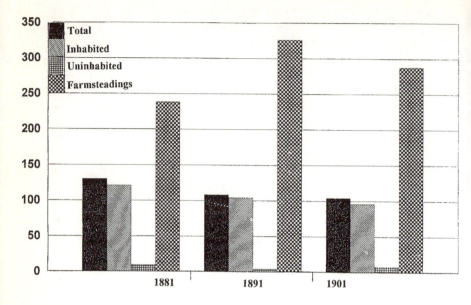

5. Buildings in Dunlavin Village 1881–1901

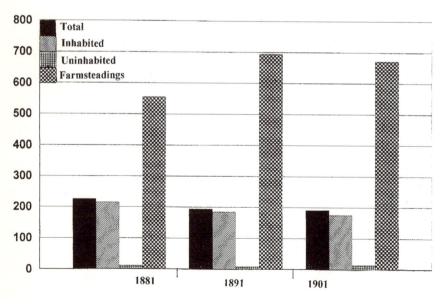

6. Buildings in Dunlavin D.E.D. 1881–1901

number of uninhabited houses remains consistently small during all three census years. There are three possible reasons for this consistently small number of uninhabited houses. Firstly, empty houses may have been tumbled quickly to clear land, and so disappeared off the landscape and off the graph. Secondly, many houses in the area contained more than one family, so out-migration may have relieved population pressure without emptying some of the houses.[27] Thirdly, empty houses may have been used as sheds by the new breed of larger tenant farmer that was emerging in the Dunlavin area at this time. These larger tenant farmers included the Moores of Tober, the Metcalfes of Crehelp and the Dwyers of Seskin.[28] If these buildings were being used as sheds, they would appear as 'out-offices and farmsteadings' on the graphs, rather than as uninhabited houses.

Despite the overall decline in inhabited houses, a trend indicating continuing out-migration during this period, sheds were being built at quite a pace during the decade from 1881 to 1891. This boom in shed building is apparent at both electoral division and village level. There are two possible explanations for this phenomenon. Firstly, tenants may not have been as reluctant to build sheds and to make improvements generally during the 1880s as agriculture recovered and they felt a greater sense of security after the land acts of 1881 and 1885 (and their later amendments). Secondly, the Tullow branch of the Great Southern and Western railway reached Dunlavin in 1885 (and Tullow in 1886).[29] Improved transportation links to outside areas, particularly to Dublin, meant that bulk buying became possible for shopkeepers in Dunlavin village and farmers in the wider electoral division, so sheds were built to store the goods purchased during this time of agricultural and economic recovery in the area. By 1901, however, the steadily diminishing population of Dunlavin was enough to ensure that the boom in the building of sheds had come to an end.[30] The 1891 population pyramid shows that total population dropped from 5,114 in 1881 to 4,394. The lower birth rates, a trend begun in the late 1870s, continued through the 1880s. In fact, the 1891 population pyramid from Dunlavin electoral division is a classic example of what demographers call a 'regressive age structure'. It shows low birth rates, indicated by its narrow base and low death rates, indicated by its steep sides below the 65–70 age group. This type of beehive-shaped population pyramid is common in modern developed areas and indicates a stable economic situation.[31] Thus although the population of Dunlavin electoral division fell between 1881 and 1891, the available wealth was being shared by fewer people so economic conditions were improving. In 1891 the non-productive sector of the population had fallen to 38 per cent, down from 41 per cent in 1881. Despite this drop, 41 per cent of the total population was still in the twenty or less age group in 1891. It would take some more years before the lower birth rates would have a significant impact on the proportion of under-twenties in the population. By 1901, however, this proportion had dropped to 36 per cent and the total population of the D.E.D. had dropped to 3,815. The rate of population decline was beginning to stabilise. The rate of decline was 13 per cent between 1891 and 1901, a slight improvement on the decline of 14 per cent recorded between 1881 and 1891. In fact the 1901 population pyramid is the most stable of the three pyramids but it is obvious that the price of demographic and economic stability in Dunlavin electoral division was continued out-migration. The years from 1881 to 1901 saw great social and economic changes within the population structure of Dunlavin electoral division. These changes were both causes and consequences of the actual population decline and, as in the case of the end of the post-railway shed-building boom, they had an adverse effect on Dunlavin village as local businesses found it harder to survive serving a declining population.[32]

Dunlavin village lay at the core of all these developments. Despite the population decline in the village during and after the Famine years, Dunlavin was still an important west Wicklow market town in the 1880s. In 1881 Dunlavin parish had a population of 4,386 and 615, or 14 per cent, of these people lived in Dunlavin village. In 1841 there had been 9,599 in the parish and 990 in the village.[33] Despite the decline in actual numbers since the Famine, the village contained a larger proportion of the parish population in 1881 and was thus relatively increasing in importance. The settlement was still a landlord-planned village with its fairgreen, market square and T-shaped street pattern. Dunlavin was a post town and its post office was also a telegraph office, a money order office and a savings bank. The post offices in the neighbouring west Wicklow villages of Donard and Stratford-on-Slaney were listed as post offices only, which indicates that Dunlavin was a higher order services centre in comparison to these adjacent settlements.[34] The village was also a market town and Wednesday was market day,[35] while the fair days in Dunlavin were on 1 March, 10 May, 16 July, 21 August, 12 October and 30 November.[36] As a market town, Dunlavin served an extensive hinterland and there was a wide variety of goods and services available in the village in 1881. In addition to basic lower order goods and services like the post office, R.I.C. station, grocery shops and pubs, Dunlavin had all the hallmarks of a stable developed settlement. There was a resident doctor, George E. Howes M.D., who had studied in Edinburgh.[37] Petty Sessions were held once a fortnight and the local magistrates were Edward Pennefather (an Oxford graduate) of Rathsallagh House and Joseph Pratt-Tynte of Tynte Park House. Tynte was a descendant of the James Worth-Tynte who had married into the Bulkeley estate in 1702, and was the biggest landlord in Dunlavin, and a dominant local figure. The clerk of the court in Dunlavin was W. R. Douglas.[38] As well as medical and legal services, the village of Dunlavin was also large enough to provide permanent banking facilities. The Munster Bank Ltd. opened a new

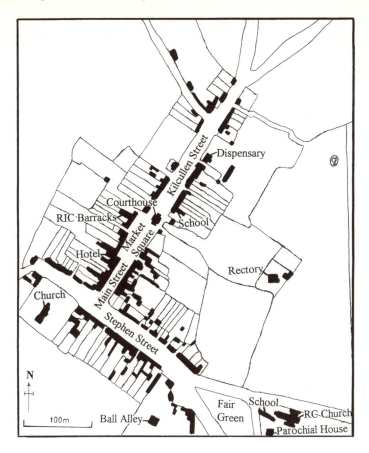

7. Dunlavin in 1898

branch in Dunlavin in 1874. The bank was described as 'a neat stone building' and Robert Crilley was the manager in 1881.[39] By 1890 this had become a branch of the Munster and Leinster Bank Ltd., open daily under the managership of A. Warmington.[40]

Dunlavin had two churches in 1881. The Protestant church was described as 'a neat plain building with a square tower' and was under the charge of Rev. J. C. Carmichael.[41] This church bears the date 1860 above the door and replaced an earlier church located in Dunlavin's market square (behind the churchyard). The Catholic church was described as 'a plain, but large and commodious structure' in 1881. This church bears the date 1898 over the door, but this was the date of major renovations and extension of the church.[42] The Catholic church in Dunlavin actually dates from 1815 according to Lord Walter

Fitzgerald,[43] who also dated the Protestant church to 1816.[44] This Protestant church does not appear on the 1838 valuation map of the village however and the building actually dates from 1860.[45] The Catholic parish priest of Dunlavin in 1881 was Canon James Whittle. Whittle was born in Dunlavin on 8 May 1818,[46] and he also held the diaconal prebend of Tassagard, an indication of the status of Dunlavin parish (and village) at the time. Whittle died on 20 March 1884, the year before the railway reached Dunlavin.

Even before the arrival of the railway, though, the village had links both within and beyond its wide hinterland. One businessman in Dunlavin in 1881 was Martin Kelly 'grocer, draper, seedsman and tallow chandler.'[47] Kelly traded with many Dublin firms including Thomas Crotty, 57 William Street, Keating and Moorehead, 17 Andrew Street and James Crotty, Hibernia Buildings, Victoria Quay. Dunlavin's cross-border links to County Kildare meant that Kelly also supplied candles to the army in the Curragh Camp.[48] Martin Kelly was only one of a number of businessmen who were making a living in Dunlavin in 1881. *Slater's Directory* for that year lists thirteen grocers and provision dealers, many of whom had other functions, such as draper, ironmonger, tallow chandler and spirit dealer listed as well. There were seven spirit dealers, as well as three public houses in the village. Other businesses to feature included two shoemakers and two saddlers. The presence of an emigration agent among the wide variety of other goods and services available in Dunlavin in 1881 reflected the ever-present reality that out-migration was a fact of life in the village at this time. In addition to business people, the directory also listed twenty-one larger farmers in the Dunlavin division of Baltinglass poor law union. These farmers formed the backbone of the Land League and, later, the National League in Dunlavin. Above the farmers on the social ladder, five people were listed as gentry, while there were three clergymen in the area. Also very high on the social scale were the six magistrates, including Joseph Pratt-Tynte of Tynte Park House, Dunlavin's dominant landlord.

In 1881 Dunlavin was a multi-functional market town serving a wide hinterland. This hinterland extended into Co. Kildare as well as Co. Wicklow and Patrick McDonough, the postmaster in Dunlavin exchanged mail with both Newbridge and Athy, while the other west Wicklow villages exchanged mail with Baltinglass, so the postal service reflected Dunlavin's cross-county links.[49] Dunlavin supplied its rural hinterland with tradesmen and craftsmen; with goods and services. The rural hinterland concentrated on agriculture and brought its produce to market in the town. This agricultural region was the domain of the strong farmers. Of the twenty-one farming families listed in *Slater's Directory* for 1881, many had held large farms (fifty or more acres) in 1854. These included the Haydens in the townland of Cowpasture, the Allens in Lugatryna, the Molyneauxs in Loughmogue Upper and Loughmogue

Lower, the Coopers in Knocknagull, the Fishers in Merginstown Glen, the Dixons and Deerings in Milltown, the Nortons in Rathsallagh and Tornant Upper and the Ennises in Tornant Lower.[50] In addition, in 1854, many of them either held or were sub-letting land in other townlands. These strong farmers had contacts throughout Dunlavin's hinterland and it was through them that mainstream political ideas like land reform and home rule were diffused into the Dunlavin area. One organisation that aspired to both home rule and land reform was the National League, a branch of which was established in Dunlavin in the 1880s. The names of these strong farmers dominated the attendance lists of National League meetings which were published in the local newspaper.[51] They also dominated the lists of speakers at National League meetings and these large farmers 'monopolised control and the expression of opinion'. This is the phrase used by P. H. Gulliver to describe the situation in Thomastown, County Kilkenny and the Dunlavin scenario was very similar during the 1880s.[52]

Most of the twenty-one leading farming families in Dunlavin in 1881 were Catholic. This suggests the existence of a wealthy rural Catholic middle class in the district, which is interesting as Fr. John Shearman had noted that anti-Catholic discrimination was the norm around Dunlavin in the 1860s. Shearman (1831–1885) was a curate in Dunlavin then and in 1862 he noted that Dunlavin Catholics had no reason to be confident about their situation as 'in general with a few exceptions they aren't wealthy, being severely tried by the ordeal of the three past inclement seasons.'[53] He recorded evictions of Catholic families in the Glen of Imaal and says that 'the district of Dunlavin has been scarcely more fortunate'.[54] Shearman himself was from a middle class Catholic background. His father, Thomas Shearman of 19, High Street, Kilkenny was a printer and publisher.[55] Shearman noted in 1862 that the Catholics in Dunlavin village itself were 'a proscribed race'.[56] He listed the nine leading Catholic families in the village as Keenan, Cunningham, Dempsy, Fay, Whittle, Dowling, Kelly and Harrington.[57] Only two of these names, Dempsy and Whittle, are absent from the *Slater's Directory* list of businesses in Dunlavin in 1881. Despite Shearman's lack of confidence the Catholic middle class in the village had consolidated its position between 1862 and 1881. However the reins of power in the Dunlavin area and in Baltinglass poor law union remained in Protestant control. The *Leinster Leader*, a nationalist newspaper, referred to the board of guardians as 'the Tory deadheads who rule the roost at Baltinglass.'[58] There is no doubt that Unionists did control Baltinglass poor law union 1890. Joseph Pratt-Tynte, the principal landlord around Dunlavin village, was an ex-officio member of the board. While he may not have attended many meetings (two in 1889 compared to sixteen meetings attended by Edward Fay, the local elected Dunlavin nationalist representative on the board),[59] Tynte's ex-officio status on the board was never threatened. Tynte had 2,532 acres in County Wicklow with a gross annual valuation of £2,186 in 1883, while other holdings in counties Dublin, Cork, Kilkenny and Leitrim brought his total estate to 5,013 acres with a valuation of £4,677.[60]

Fay, on the other hand, was a member of a prominent Catholic family in Dunlavin. The Catholic merchant community had strengthened its position. In the 1860s the Fays were among the nine leading Catholic families in Dunlavin village. The leading Catholic family, the Harringtons, had a valuation of £136 10s.[61] The gulf between the Protestant landlord class and the Catholic middle class was obviously wide in late nineteenth-century Dunlavin. Edward Fay, a grocer and spirit dealer,[62] was elected as Poor Law Guardian in 1888. He was the first Catholic to represent Dunlavin in this position and had the support of the politically minded strong tenant farmers in the district.[63] Strong tenant farmers, in their turn, were well below the local landlords on the social ladder. Joseph Pratt-Tynte, who was born in 1815 and married to Geraldine Northey of Cheltenham in 1840,[64] was a resident landlord, living at Tynte Park House, about two miles from Dunlavin village.[65] The house was built in the 1830s and was described as 'a splendid mansion and out-offices.'[66] The Tynte estate was the thirty-seventh largest (by acreage) in County Wicklow in 1876,[67] and Tynte Park was a far cry from the houses occupied by the tenant farmers, even the strong ones, in a county where 29 per cent of the houses were still listed as third or fourth class as late as 1891.[68] Tynte was also a local magistrate and the landlord presence in Dunlavin was strong. The Catholic middle class was not yet a threat to the control wielded in the area by Tynte and others of the landlord class. The relative positions of the two Poor Law Guardians, Tynte and Fay, demonstrated where the power lay within Baltinglass poor law union. This situation was unpalatable to the nationalist *Leinster Leader*, but was nonetheless a fait accompli in late nineteenth-century Dunlavin.

Tynte was a leading figure in Dunlavin Church of Ireland circles and is buried in the local churchyard.[69] He was a wealthy member of the gentry, but even below the level of the gentry there were imbalances between lifestyles and opportunities afforded to Protestants and Catholics in late nineteenth-century Dunlavin. One area where this is obvious is that of education. In 1881 Dunlavin had a Protestant school under the care of the Master Charles O'Connor, and had separate male and female national schools, attended by Catholic children, with two principals, Master Thomas Grace and Miss Toomey respectively.[70] There were actually six schools under Catholic management in Dunlavin parish in the 1880s, the others being co-educational schools in Donard, Merginstown, Davidstown and Seskin.[71] Despite the numerical superiority of Catholic schools, Protestant children were better educated, or at least more literate, than their Catholic counterparts. In 1881 the Protestant population of Dunlavin comprised 21 per cent of the village total. There was a very high literacy rate among the Protestant population who were over five years old – 92 per cent. Only 4 per cent of the Protestant males and 4 per cent of Protestant females were illiterate in 1881. In contrast, the illiteracy rate for Catholics who were over five years old stood at 22 per cent in 1881. About one Protestant in twelve could not read or write, but almost one Catholic in four could not. Again there was an even breakdown between the sexes, with 11 per cent of the males and 11 per cent of females being illiterate. Obviously the Catholic schools were not as effective as the Protestant one. It is possible that the Protestant school was slightly better equipped with books and other educational aids like maps and charts, but it is more probable that the lower effectiveness of the Catholic schools had its root in the socio-economic conditions of the Catholics in Dunlavin at this time. The Catholic middle class was becoming more confident and outward looking at this time, but below them there was a poorer class of small tenant farmers and manual labourers. These were the people who occupied the third and fourth class houses, and their socio-economic background meant that they were likely to place a low value on education. Their children were at risk of being kept at home from school to help out at home, playing truant and of leaving school at a very early age. These poorer Catholics probably accounted for the bulk of the 22 per cent of illiterates.[72] They also formed a kind of underclass in the village and its environs during the twenty-year period from 1881–1901.

Thus Dunlavin, the west Wicklow market town serving both an upland and a lowland hinterland, was a village which had a declining population during this period, but the rate of decline was stabilising. There was some class tension, and as the Catholic middle class strengthened and grew in confidence they became interested and involved in local politics. It was the larger tenant farmers however who dominated this arena in Dunlavin, so the Catholic lower class in the district did not gain much from the activities of organisations such as the National League, despite lip service being paid to the plight of the labourers.[73] Along with social class, religion was another divisive force in local politics. The avowed aim of the Land League was reform of the landholding system. In practice, in Dunlavin, this included an attack on Protestant landlords such as Tynte and his peers. For the Catholic middle class to emerge as stronger players on the local scene in Dunlavin, control would have to be wrested from the Protestant landlord class. Religion and politics were two important factors in Dunlavin life in the late nineteenth century. Often intertwined, it is these two threads of village life, seen through the eyes of Fr. Donovan, that form the basis for the remainder of this study.

Donovan's parish: religion in Dunlavin 1881–1901

The village of Dunlavin contained two religious communities in the late nineteenth century. Two churches, Roman Catholic and Church of Ireland, stood at either end of the village. The members of each Church had much in common, but also had different life experiences. Two sources reflect this very well – Canon Donovan's unpublished diary and the Church of Ireland's rector McGee's published *Retrospect*. This chapter will draw on these two sources to explore some of the similarities and differences recorded by these clergymen.

The Roman Catholic church in Dunlavin dates from 1815 and in that year Lady Hannah Tynte-Caldwell donated the site to the Catholic parish. A plaque acknowledging this event was erected in the church.[1] In fact, the site had previously been used for Catholic worship as Fr. Shearman recorded 'St. Nicholas of Myra church is now the parish church and was rebuilt on the old site about 1815'.[2] A further indication that the year 1815 marked a new beginning is the fact that surviving parish registers date from that year and the first entries record the baptisms of three infants – Michael Brien, Hannah Healy and Michael Magarr – on 1 October 1815.[3] By 1837 the Catholic church was described as a 'neat cruciform edifice.'[4] In the pre-Famine era the numbers worshipping in the church were very high. In 1834 Dunlavin parish had a population of 2,104 Catholics with 700–1,000 attending the first mass and nearly 2,000 attending the second mass in 1835.[5] The Catholic church in Dunlavin continued to serve a large congregation in the post-Famine years. In 1862, in addition to the parishioners of Dunlavin 'a large concourse attended from Uske and Gormanstown in County Kildare'.[6] Also in 1862 Fr. James Whittle came to Dunlavin as parish priest.[7] Whittle served as parish priest of Dunlavin until his death on 20 March 1884. He was a native of Dunlavin, born on 8 May 1818, and baptised in the local church on 10 May.[8] Whittle, who had studied in Maynooth, succeeded Very Rev. John Hyland as parish priest on 8 November 1862 and was inducted at 12 o'clock mass on the following Sunday by Venerable Archdeacon Lawrence Dunne, the parish priest of Castledermot, at the request of Most Rev. Dr. Paul Cullen, archbishop of Dublin.[9] During Whittles's tenure as parish priest, a number of building projects were undertaken by the parish. In 1873 a new coach house and stables were constructed beside the parochial house at a cost of £142 6s. 7d. In 1880 a new schoolhouse was constructed within the chapel yard at Dunlavin. However, by far the largest project undertaken in Whittle's time was the construction of a new church at Davidstown. This church (of our Lady of Dolours and St. Patrick) was officially opened on 16 September 1875. It was obviously an expensive undertaking and Whittle listed the expenses, the largest being £75 to the architect and £1,567 to the builder.[10] By 1880 then, despite Whittle's extensive building programme, the Church of St. Nicholas of Myra in Dunlavin remained relatively untouched and unchanged. Whittle listed a number of running repairs done to the church – roof repairs, walls plastered, windows repaired – but these were only stopgap measures. Apart from the purchasing of a set of Stations of the Cross for the interior of the church, the building was not substantially altered during Whittle's tenure.

Whittle died on 20 March 1884.[11] He was succeeded as parish priest on 17 April 1884 by Rev. Frederick Augustine Donovan. Donovan was born in Dublin on 18 May 1830. He matriculated on 12 February 1850 and entered Maynooth College. He was ordained on 6 June 1857 by Archbishop Paul Cullen.[12] Donovan's first appointment was as locum tenens in Celbridge, where he remained from 27 June to 25 November 1857. He then received a curacy in Arklow, under Canon Redmond, where he remained until he was appointed to Dunlavin. Donovan had secured a parish for himself, but in 1884 the physical fabric of Dunlavin parish and the buildings in particular were in need of urgent attention. In fact, right from the beginning of Donovan's tenure in the village it is obvious that the church, parochial house and schools were in a bad state of repair. In 1884 the parochial house was repaired at a cost of £109. Also in 1884, Donovan turned his attention to the Dunlavin male and female national schools. He referred to them as 'mere wrecks of buildings' and had a substantial repair job done on them. The buildings were 'dashed, ceiled, whitened, cemented, painted, furnished with eve gutters and downpipes and the out-offices rebuilt at a cost of £48.' Donovan also obtained a grant of £6 for school equipment from the Commissioners of National Education. A new missal and stand were purchased for the church at a cost of £1 16s. By the end of 1884 Donovan had begun to make his mark in Dunlavin parish. The parochial house and schools had been repaired, but the church building remained untouched. One of Donovan's curates, Rev. Thomas A. Brennan had been moved to Balbriggan in November 1884 and he was replaced by Rev. Peter Vallely from Delgany. Donovan's other curate, Rev. Thomas Lynch, had been there in Whittle's time and, with Whittle, was responsible for the building of the new church in Davidstown. Lynch remained in Donard, serving the upland portion of the parish.

Dunlavin Catholic parish now boasted three churches, two parochial houses and six schools, but this fact caused constant maintenance worries and expenses. Donovan recorded many repairs and some improvements to these buildings during his years in Dunlavin, but one senses that many of these were (as in Whittle's time) stopgap measures or were only undertaken because things had become so bad that they had to be done – particularly from 1890 onwards. Donovan's improvements to the interior of the church, as well as his liturgical purchases of chalices, vestments etc. added a sense of majesty to the mass and other services, thus making Donovan an important agent in extending the 'devotional revolution' in Dunlavin. Such an agent needed a comfortable residence and in February 1885 David Rankin of Naas installed a new fireplace in Dunlavin parochial house. His costs, along with bricks, cement, lime, labour and carriage totalled £12 2s. In August 1885 Merginstown national school was repaired. The building was 'plastered and ceiled and a new gate was erected'. Donovan noted thankfully that the £15 outlay meant that the school was entitled to a £3 equipment grant.

One improvement that was made to the church in Dunlavin in August 1885 however did not spare expense. This was the erection of a memorial side aisle altar to the memory of Donovan's predecessor, Canon Whittle. Donovan referred to it as 'a handsome structure composed of Caen stone, Italian and French marble and Devonshire spar with a wrought-iron and brass tabernacle.' The architect was William Hague and his fee was £5, while the total cost of the altar was £61 5s. 6d. Donovan hired a new sculptor for this job. Work on the new church in Davidstown was carried out by the Dublin sculptors, P. J. Neill and Co. They had been hired in Whittle's time. Donovan, however, hired the Dublin firm of Pearse and Sharp to erect the memorial altar to Whittle. This was the firm of Patrick Pearse's father.[13] It is possible that the Dublin-born nationalist Donovan knew the Pearse family before he moved to Dunlavin. In October 1885, Pearse and Sharp also erected 'a mural tablet with the inscription on white marble, framed in Caen stone and black marble, the whole neat and graceful' to Whittle's memory. This cost £19. However, the cost of the memorial to Whittle was well covered by the £116 8s. collected in the Canon Whittle memorial fund. Donovan recorded the names of 109 subscribers to the fund. Subscriptions varied from 5 guineas (Donovan himself) to 5 shillings (thirty-one subscribers). After Donovan, the leading local individual Catholic subscriber was John Harrington of Cannycourt with £5. The average subscription was £1 5s. 2d., and on the list the names of strong farmers (Deering and Norton for example) and local businessmen (Kelly and Fay for example) are to the fore, but some prominent local Protestant names like Pennefather, Mahony and Dixon are also present. Tynte's name is absent, but Donovan tells us that 'protestant gentlemen have been among the foremost in generously testifying their appreciation of his [Whittle's] amiable character and virtues.' The wide range of donations suggests that subscribers came from all social strata.

While the erection of Whittle's memorial altar enhanced the interior of Dunlavin church, the building itself was still in need of repair. In December 1885, Donovan paid £15 to Waldrons (listed as slaters and plasterers in

Dunlavin in *Slater's Directory* of 1881) for 'dashing, painting of windows and doors and roof slating.' In July 1886 the church windows were repaired again, at a cost of £4 1s., while the church bell was moved 'as the belfry was in a very decayed and dangerous condition. New materials of wood and metal were supplied and the whole frame painted at a cost of £11'. In August 1886 the interior of the church was painted 'with much care and skill' by Martin Cooke of Grangecon, while Thomas Kirwan of Uppertown partially concreted the floor which had been in a bad condition. These jobs cost £26. As one maintenance job finished, another started. Donard church was repaired by Waldrons of Dunlavin – walls dashed and painted, windows and doors also painted – at a cost of £34 in September 1886. The upkeep of three churches was an expensive business, and equipment had to be bought as well. Also in August 1887, Donovan purchased new candlesticks lamps and vases for Dunlavin church, but in March 1887 he had managed to reduce the cost of a ten-guinea chalice by trading in his old one for £3 10s., thus only paying £7 for the new one. Nurturing the devotional revolution was obviously no reason to abandon the virtue of thrift! Despite this thrift the new high altar in Davidstown church was completed in May 1887. It consisted of 'Caen stone with pillars of coloured marbles and the altar table and candle benches of Sicilian marble, gracefully designed by Mr. William Haugue.' P. J. Neill and Co. Dublin (who had worked on Davidstown church for Whittle) carried out this work at a cost of £107. The new church at Davidstown was causing an extra financial strain in Dunlavin parish at this time.

The schools also needed investment. In October 1887 'twelve desks of superior construction in varnished pine with metal standards made by Scott and Co. Dublin' arrived in Dunlavin school at a cost of £19 10s. The school floor also had to be repaired and the walls were whitewashed, bringing the total cost to £21 4s., while in December of that year a new harmonium costing £5 5s. was purchased for the female national school 'to encourage musical taste and help supply singers for the choir'. September 1888 saw £30 3s. paid out for 'large and important repairs' to Seskin national school. The cost would have been much more but Donovan noted thankfully that 'men, horses, cars and sand were supplied free', thereby making a considerable saving of expenditure possible. The ceiling and walls of Davidstown national school were also repaired at a cost of £1 at this time. By September 1888 the new church in Davidstown was also in need of repair. The old plaster on the chancel was removed and cemented, and the back of the altar was painted at a cost of £5. Once built, the church at Davidstown also needed maintenance and this is the first of a number of repairs carried out there, placing an extra strain on parish finances. Two sets of violet vestments for Dunlavin church (£3 10s.) and a new harmonium for Donard church (£8) added to the parochial outlay in 1888. Once again many stopgap jobs were undertaken in 1889. These included painting whitewashing and glazing the Dunlavin schools once again

(£3 6s. 8d.), putting up altar railings in Davidstown (£17 8s.) and repairing the roof of Donard church (£1 7s.) in June; roof repairs to Dunlavin sacristy (£24 1s.) in August; the building of a coal-house for Seskin N.S. (£16 15s.) in September and painting the gutters of Davidstown church (£2) in December.

The upkeep of the new church at Davidstown and the other parochial buildings was obviously taking its toll. In December 1890 Donovan recorded that 'parish expenditure was designedly very limited this year.' Davidstown church was painted (£3 4s.), Dunlavin bell frame and seats were repaired (£1 1s.), a new stove (£1 11s. 6d.) and a statue of St. Joseph (£1 12s.) were purchased. Nothing else is recorded for 1890. In 1891 Donovan's diary records that 'church expenses and parochial outlay were again very limited.' In fact, total expenditure that year came only to some £13 or £14. There is no record of the parochial bank balance at this time, but the lean years of 1890 and 1891 suggest that the balance at this time was not too healthy. There had been heavy parochial outlay during he 1880s and it is possible that the limited expenditure of 1890 and 1891 was at the behest of A. Warmington, the bank manager in Dunlavin. This trend continued in 1892, when Donovan recorded that 'parochial expenditure on church and school improvements this year were of the most nominal character', the highest cost being £2 8s. 10d. for a new stove. If the parish had overspent during the 1880s it was making up for it in the early 1890s!

By 1893 however, something had to be done about the condition of Dunlavin church and schools. During June, July and August a 'large work was executed in Dunlavin'. Church and school walls were cemented and dashed and a sewerage system was installed in both national schools. This involved laying pipes across Dunlavin fairgreen and along the yard of the parochial house. These improvements cost £70, but once again Donovan was very thankful for free sand and labour. Local merchant Edward Fay's expenditure on this venture was written off, another indication that times were hard for the parish. Donovan recorded that other expenses that year were very limited – organ tuning (£1 10s. 6d.), drainage at Seskin school (£1 2s. 6d.) and repairing a broken monstrance (12s. 6d.) being the most expensive items. The expensive repairs of the summer of 1893 were not repeated in 1894, and in December of that year Donovan noted in his diary that 'there was no parochial outlay during the course of the year.' The new Davidstown school opened in 1894, vested under five trustees – Dr. Walsh, archbishop of Dublin, Fr. Donovan and the three vicars general, Monsignors Walsh, Fitzpatrick and Plunkett – but no parochial money was spent on the new school that year. The parochial accounts were still severely strained in 1894. In May 1895 the new school was inspected and passed. The £300 cost of the school was met by a grant of £175 12s. 8d. from the National Board, a 'handsome figure' from the Imaal loan fund, a 'very liberal subscription' from Archbishop Walsh and local contributions of about £30 due to the 'very considerable personal exertions of the P.P.' No other expenses are recorded for 1895 and Donovan's diary ends with the entry on 30 September for that year.

Donovan died on 15 December 1896,[14] but there are no entries in his diary for that year, so it is possible that he was in bad health for about a year before his death. He was succeeded by Fr. John Maxwell,[15] who was appalled at the state of Dunlavin church when he arrived. At a meeting of parishioners held on 8 September 1898, Maxwell stated that 'he was surprised and grieved when he came to Dunlavin and saw such a miserable, poor and dangerous church. It was nothing short of a disgrace to religion and altogether unfit for divine worship. The galleries were in a fearful state, being supported by rotten beams, a portion of the ceiling was also in a most dilapidated condition and the wonder was why some of the parishioners had not been killed or maimed'.[16] Maxwell proposed a major renovation and extension of the church and pledged that all labour on the job would come from Dunlavin itself. Michael Roche of Dunlavin undertook to 'thoroughly renovate the church for the sum of £1,300', while Mr. Waldron, 'a Protestant and a thoroughly good workman into the bargain' would also get a share of the work. Donovan had left £1,000 toward a new church in Dunlavin in his will, but the words 'new church' made it difficult to obtain the money for renovating the existing building, although legal moves to procure the money were afoot. Even with Donovan's £1,000 however, the cost of such a major job would be considerably more than the amount of money in the parish coffers at the time, so a fund was opened to collect money for the venture.[17] The extension of the church was carried out and the date 1898 may still be seen over the main door of the extended long aisle and below the new belfry. Ornamental railings replaced the outside wall and Dunlavin church was much altered by the dawn of the twentieth century. This renovation of the church was undertaken as part of the centenary commemoration of the events of 1798 in the parish of Dunlavin. Stained glass windows commemorating the massacre on Dunlavin green and the rebel leader Michael Dwyer were to be put into the church.[18] This, however, was never done.

One of the earlier entries in Donovan's diary, dated 5 July 1885 records that: 'on 11 February Cardinal McCabe expired. On the following 10 March, the canons and parish priests of Dublin diocese by an overwhelming majority selected Dr. William Walsh, president of Maynooth College as his successor, and after a period of painful suspense owing to English intrigues at Rome, to the great joy of the Irish nation the selection was ratified by His Holiness.' The basis of British objections to Walsh was his ultra nationalistic stance.[19] Donovan, however, was elated at Walsh's appointment and stood four square behind the new bishop. On 26 September 1885 Walsh travelled to Kilcullen to consecrate the new high altar in Kilcullen church. He was greeted by the Crehelp brass band and the town was bedecked with green flags, laurels, evergreen arches and nationalist banners, some of which read: 'Kilcullen branch of the National League greets you with *Cead Mile Failte*', 'The Just shall be in Everlasting Remembrance', 'Our God and Our Country', 'Home Rule', 'Tenant Right', 'Faith and Fatherland', and 'Ireland a Nation'.[20] Donovan was one of three neighbouring parish priests who travelled to Kilcullen to read addresses to Walsh. Of the four addresses delivered to Walsh the following day, 27 September, Donovan's is by far the most overtly political, making reference to

> The joy we experienced when we learned of the overthrow of statecraft and intrigue, and the triumph of religious independence in the confirmation by the Holy See of the free choice of our Irish Church. We believed you are not alone a true churchman, but a true patriot as well and we were not mistaken.

The address went on to speak of the 'effects of centuries of misrule' and express the hope that the work of 'capable representatives in parliament' will see the return of prosperity and 'evil traditions forgotten.'[21] Donovan led a deputation of prominent Dunlaviners that day – John Harrington, Thomas Norton, Anthony Metcalfe P.L.G. and James Cunningham, and their address was published in a book of Walsh's addresses in 1886, a work which was sanctioned by Walsh himself.[22] The other addresses, from Kilcullen, Ballymore and Hollywood and Castledermot were also published, but were less nationalistic in tone. Donovan recorded in his diary that he had delivered a 'congratulatory address' to the new archbishop.

Donovan's overt nationalistic views were evident again when he chaired a 'large and enthusiastic meeting' on Tornant moat on 22 November 1885 in support of Garret Byrne, one of the nationalist candidates in the County Wicklow election of that year. This was 'the first public meeting that he had ever presided at – it was not his ambition to preside at public meetings but he did so as it was gratifying to the people and useful to the cause.' Donovan undoubtedly realised the weight that was carried by his position as parish priest of Dunlavin. The priest, an educated figure at a time when a high proportion of the population of Dunlavin left school at an early age, was an important figurehead in the parish. Even the curates carried considerable authority and status. When Rev. Thomas Lynch, curate of Donard, died (aged 44) on 20 May 1887, Donovan recorded that there were twenty-six priests assembled for the requiem mass and nineteen for the month's memory. Donovan noted that Lynch was ' very zealous and highly popular with the people owing to his simple, homely and genial nature'.

Rev. Patrick Brennan, newly ordained from Maynooth college succeeded Lynch in June 1887. The raw Brennan accepted a gift of a horse and car from his parishioners to help with the 'expenses of a priest's first mission', but Donovan told him that this contravened an existing church statute. Many areas of clerical life were tightened up at the Synod of Thurles in 1850 and again at the Synod of Maynooth in 1875.[23] Brennan wrote to Archbishop Walsh, asking if he could keep the horse and car.[24] There is no record of Walsh's reply! This incident shows another side to Donovan. The middle-class, meticulous, nationalistic parish priest also knew his church law and was at pains to point it out to his young curate. Brennan left Donard in December 1888, but not before the death of another curate, this time Fr. Peter Vallely of Dunlavin. Vallely died suddenly on 3 March in the parochial house, from 'heart disease' according to the inquest. Donovan's diary lists twenty-eight priests who celebrated the funeral mass before Vallely was interred in a suite of coffins–shell, lead and oak – beside Canon Whittle in the nave of Dunlavin church. Vallely, who was 'quiet, gentle and unassuming in manner' according to Donovan, was replaced on 14 March 1888 by Rev. Christopher Grimes, while Rev. John Hickey succeeded Brennan in Donard on 1 December.

The ex-curate of Donard Thomas Lynch had left £50 in his will to the Catholic poor of Donard, but only £28 8s. 9d. was distributed in June 1889 due to insufficient assets. Donovan too was involved in good works and charitable causes. On 27 May 1890 Donovan recorded the entry of four orphans – Patrick, Michael, Joseph and Thomas Kennedy – into Artane industrial school. He undertook to pay each one an extra 6d. per week on top of the grand jury county payment. This was at a time when 'parochial expenditure was designedly very limited' and shows a kind side to Donovan's nature, which is unrecorded elsewhere even in his meticulous diary. The meticulous side of Donovan's nature again emerged in 1891 when he painstakingly recorded the census details for Dunlavin parish. He noted a decrease of 638 people since 1881 and also noted the religious breakdown of the parish, 2,809 Catholics (1,422 in Dunlavin and 1,387 in Donard) and 939 Protestants. There is no doubt that the almost 70 per cent of the people who made up the Catholic population of Dunlavin parish held their parish priest in high esteem. Donovan was appointed Vicar Forane on 18 June 1890, and elevated to the status of canon on 10 January 1893. On 12 March 1893 Donovan was presented with an address on behalf of his parishioners. The address referred in glowing terms to Donovan's better traits and stated that he was 'true to the traditions of the Soggarth Aroon'. It referred to 'the crowded confessionals, the flourishing state of the Sacred Heart, Purgatorian and Living Rosary sodalites, the high answering of the school children at both the religious and secular examinations, the whole tone of the community under your charge . . . all tell of the guiding spirit that directs and controls God's beneficent machinery in this faithful old parish of Dunlavin, Donard and Donaghmore'. In his reply, Donovan stated that the committee of John Harrington, James O'Connor M.P., Francis McEnerny C.C. (who had replaced Grimes in December 1889), Henry Copeland, Anthony Metcalfe, John Fallon, John Rochfort, James Cunningham and Thomas Metcalfe 'worthily represent the parish. Here beside me is the cultured churchman. Then we have the prosperous grazier and enterprising mercantile speculator.

We also have the local merchant, the farmer and the skilled artisan among you. All classes are here worthily represented.' This cross section of the classes in Dunlavin parish mentioned by Donovan indicates that their Catholicism was a unifying force. The post-Famine Catholic church was the product of the 'devotional revolution', a term first used by the historian Emmet Larkin.[25] Whether the Famine was the cause or the catalyst of this phenomenon is uncertain,[26] but there certainly is evidence that devotional practice was very strong in Dunlavin parish during the late nineteenth century. Even before Donovan's arrival in Dunlavin, Canon Whittle had noted that the ten-day mission conducted by two Jesuits, Fathers Flynn and Cleary in 1880 was 'admirably conducted by the fathers and well attended by the people'.[27]

Donovan's diary contains more evidence of a devotional parish. Another Jesuit mission was held from 11 October to 1 November 1885. The Jesuits, John Gaffney and William Fortescue, spent the first fortnight in Dunlavin and the third week in Donard. Donovan noted happily that 2,400 people received communion – 1,500 in Dunlavin and 900 in Donard. There were 3,349 Catholics in the parish in 1881, but the population pyramid reveals that almost 1,000 of these were less than ten years of age, so the figure of 2,400 communicants represents virtually a 100 per cent attendance. According to Donovan 'the people attended various duties with much quiet fervour and steadiness. The fathers delivered earnest and instructive discourses and were assiduous in their confessional labours and the mission was decidedly a complete success.' This is one area of Donovan's diary where caution must be advised however. He saw the mission through the eyes of a parish priest, and his account naturally reflects this. It is not deliberate bias, but other studies of nineteenth and early twentieth-century missions in rural areas suggest that an account written by a lay person who attended the mission might differ from Donovan's view. Laurence J. Taylor wrote of 'locals revealing in their own accounts of missions a different sort of religious experience from that intended by the missionaries'.[28] Alice Taylor goes further when she writes 'To me, the missioner on the altar provided a one man entertainment'.[29]

Whatever about the quality of religious experience received at the mission however, the fact remains that the Dunlavin missions were very well attended. Formal devotional practice was very important in Dunlavin and in August 1886 the village braced itself to welcome its archbishop, Dr. Walsh, for confirmation. On 23 August, Walsh arrived in Dunlavin railway station on the 11.05 a.m. train to confirm 279 children. He and his chaplain, Fr. Pettit, were

> welcomed by the people in the handsomest and most enthusiastic manner. The Crehelp brass band and the Donard fife and drum band played patriotic music and the children gaily attired walked in procession. The people cheered His Grace as he advanced slowly seated in Mr. J. Harrington's open carriage under triumphal green arches.

John Harrington had a large landholding in Cannycourt, just over the Kildare border from Dunlavin. He was also the chairman of the committee who presented Donovan with the address to mark his elevation to the status of canon, and was a leading member of the local Catholic community, as well as being deeply involved in the National League (see next chapter). Harrington's coach bore Dr. Walsh through the streets, 'banners and bannerets floated in the breeze, and flags in great profusion waved from the windows'. Having reached the church Walsh confirmed the children. The notes that he made for that confirmation sermon in 1886 have survived. The sermon was addressed to 'My dear children' and as one reads through them, it becomes obvious that this term includes the whole congregation, not just those about to be confirmed. The whole tone of the sermon made it clear that Walsh was a figure of authority. He told the candidates for confirmation to

> Excite every feeling of piety within your hearts, for upon the fervour of devotion with which you receive it now may depend whether you are to be admitted for all eternity to a place among the angels around the throne of God in heaven, or to be cast out forever from his sight and from the company of his holy angels to spend an eternity of pain and sorrow among the devils in hell.'[30]

After the confirmation Donovan recorded that 'the little town was brilliantly illuminated and tar barrels blazed upon the green'. Overall however, Donovan noted that the confessionals and altar rails were full and the people acted as 'docile children of the Catholic Church' during that Jubilee year of 1886.

While the arrival of missioners and the bishop were very well attended, they constituted special events in the parish. However smaller events were important also. On 22 July 1888 a forty hours adoration and retreat for the members of the Sacred Heart Association was 'well conducted by Rev. J. B. Leybourn O.C.C., and well attended'. In May 1890 the parish Total Abstinence Association was established and 296 juveniles took the pledge until they were twenty-one years old, while 327 adults also took the pledge. On 29 July of that year a further 297 confirmation candidates were added to the number of juveniles. Confirmation numbers continued to be high, and it was not until August 1894, when only 203 children were confirmed, that the confirmation numbers began to reflect the fall in the birth rate which had occurred in the 1880s. Despite diminishing numbers, in 1891 Donovan recorded that 'quiet and order reigned through the peaceful parish as usual during the year. The sacraments were frequented and the sodality meetings largely attended'. Devotional practice was whipped into another fervour by a further mission, this time held by three Vincentians, from 24 July to 15 August 1892. Frs. Daniel O'Sullivan, Louis Bean and Daniel McCarthy spent the first half of the mission in Dunlavin and the second in Donard. 'The mission was eminently successful, the various exercises were admirably attended by the faithful and the sermons were forceful and fruitful of result. The people came in large numbers from all the neighbouring parishes. The mission was entirely free and not one penny was charged. 2,710 communions were the distributed, 1,460 in Dunlavin and 1,250 in Donard'. Once again these figures represent practically the whole Catholic parish at that time.

When Donovan received the canonical address from his parishioners on 12 March 1893, there seems little doubt that the passage relating to the 'crowded confessionals, flourishing sodalities and God's beneficent machinery in this faithful old parish' was a true reflection of a parish which had a high degree of devotional practice at that time. Yet, beneath the surface there was a different picture. There were twenty-six illegitimate births recorded in the parish register between 1881 and 1901. The figure of 1.3 per cent per annum is very low, but it did exist. The social stigma of illegitimacy was hard to bear at the time. Some mothers moved to other areas to have their children. In 1886 Donovan recorded 'This child's mother is a stranger from the neighbourhood of Kilcullen town and only lived in Crehelp for about one week before the birth.'[31] Despite the high level of devotional practice, the message of the fire and brimstone sermons was obviously not getting through to everyone, nor did it control all areas of Catholic life. Another sort of religiosity in the parish which was less under the control of the resurgent Catholic Church was the widespread practice of folk-religion. The major area of folk religion in Dunlavin centred on St. Nicholas's holy well at Tornant. In 1862 Shearman noted that 'this well at Tornant was the scene of one of the most famed mid-Leinster patterns. St. John's eve was the day on which the pattern began and it lasted for three days. Tents and booths were erected and the crowds came from Carlow, Athy and from the farthest parts of the King's County. It was one of the leading patterns in the whole country, but owing to the great abuses and riots consequent on these gatherings, the owner of the land Mr. Ennis and the P.P. Fr. John Hyland ultimately abolished it.'[32] Hyland, who preceded Whittle as parish priest of Dunlavin and died in 1862,[33] may have abolished the pattern, but that was not the end of the matter. The pattern did not die (although Donovan studiously ignored it in his diary) and people continued to seek cures. Crutches, walking sticks and pieces of cloth were left at the well in the 1880s.[34] People arrived by train to do the pattern in late June. The railway only reached Dunlavin in 1885, and the arrival of pilgrims by train continued into the twentieth century when 'lots of people streamed across local fields to pray at our well.'[35] The pattern to the well survived in spite of the efforts of the Catholic clergy to suppress it on grounds of drunkenness and faction fighting.[36] Children were bathed in the well and one unusual aspect of this practice in Dunlavin was that both Catholic and Protestant children were 'dipped'.[37]

Nearly one third of the population of Dunlavin parish was Protestant in 1891 according to Donovan's figures. The Protestant population of the area had a different religious experience to their Catholic counterparts. A new rector, Samuel Russell McGee, arrived on Easter Sunday 1894. McGee was born in 1856 into a well-to-do family.[38] He became curate of Clontarf in 1888 and was asked to become rector of Dunlavin in 1894. He accepted, but found that his new rectory was uninhabitable. He wrote: 'the rectory was an impossible proposition without the expenditure of a large sum of money; it was the worst glebe house but one [in the diocese]. The lawn was a forest of large trees.'[39] McGee faced similar problems to Donovan on his arrival in Dunlavin, with both his house and his church in bad repair. Fortunately the parish had a trust fund which had been created by the landowning parishioners who had levied themselves on the basis of their rental income since 1871. As the rector at the time, Archdeacon J. O'Regan, was a pre-disestablishment cleric, the fund couldn't be touched till after his death, which occurred in 1880. Thus there was money to renovate the rectory and the trustees, Col. Tynte C.B., E. Pennefather Q.C., T. Molyneaux J.P. and R. Dixon J.P. agreed to use the money for that purpose. The work took longer than expected as rain caused all the ceilings to collapse during re-slating, but the rectory was ready for use and free of debt by August 1894.[40]

As with the Catholic community, the Church of Ireland community of Dunlavin also found that maintenance of buildings was a never ending job and a constant struggle. In 1895 the church was in need of repair and once again local tradesmen were employed. Joseph Waldron, a Protestant, and Michael Roche, a Catholic, carried out the repair work. They were to take on a major renovation of the Catholic church in Dunlavin three years later as we have seen. Religion did not seem to be a barrier to these jobs as both churches were repaired by men of both faiths and in each case the local clergy seemed happy to take on local labour. Maxwell commented on this in 1898 and McGee recorded that in a town of only 400 people it was possible to find men to do nearly all the work on both the rectory and the church, and Waldron and Roche did 'excellent work.'[41] The church had to be closed for three months, but was re-opened by the archbishop of Dublin, Lord Plunket on 20 August 1895. McGee recorded that there was a 'very large' congregation that day, and the new seating in the church (donated by Tynte) was thronged. The jewels in the crown of the renovation work were the new pitch pine ceiling and new choir stalls.[42] The archbishop's address mentioned the increased effort that had to be made by members of the Church of Ireland since disestablishment in 1869. Gladstone's Disestablishment Act resulted in loss of income at grass roots level and Plunket congratulated the Dunlavin congregation on their support for the renovation and beautification of their church. This beauty, he said, 'did not indicate in any sense a craving after ritualistic display, nor betoken a return towards those dangerous innovations which at the Reformation their church disowned and rejected'. In Dunlavin Plunket said that he found 'order, decency, beauty and dignity.'[43] He then confirmed about thirty young people (a contrast to the vast numbers for confirmation in the Catholic church). The religious service was followed by what McGee refers to as an 'at home' at the rectory, which hosted a 'very large gathering of parishioners and their friends'.[44] The rectory was obviously now fit to house such an event, unlike the situation in 1894 when it was 'looked upon as anything but a prize'.[45] The trust fund set up on the motion of Andrew Dixon and seconded by Joseph Molyneaux in 1871, that 'Protestant proprietors of the parish pay 1s. in the pound on lands in their own occupation and 6d. in the pound on lands and premises occupied by Roman Catholic tenants and that Protestant tenants pay 6d. in the pound on lands and premises occupied by them for the maintenance of the future minister of Dunlavin,'[46] had borne fruit by 1895 and Dunlavin could now boast a fine rectory and church.

Dr. Peacocke, who succeeded Plunket as archbishop of Dublin, referred to Dunlavin as 'one of the nicest country churches in the diocese' in 1899.[47] By then however, more work had been carried out on the church, chiefly to commemorate three of its main benefactors, all of whom died between 1895 and 1899. In 1895 Edward Pennefather Q.C. of Rathsallagh House, 'one of our ablest lawyers and a churchman of intense loyalty', died. His death was followed in 1896 by the death of Joseph Pratt-Tynte of Tynte Park House 'who for fifty-six years, to a great extent, presided over the destinies of Dunlavin parish and district.'[48] McGee's words sum up the situation as to where local power lay. Tynte, the landlord of the village, did control its destiny, but that control was under pressure by the final decade of the nineteenth century. It was decided by the parishioners that both Pennefather and Tynte, who had served the church as diocesan synodsmen,[49] should be commemorated in the church. Both families were consulted and a memorial chancel was commissioned. Peacocke consecrated the chancel on 22 December 1897. McGee listed ten clergy who were present in their robes at the service. The service was followed by a reception in Tynte Park House given by the new owner, Tynte's son and heir Colonel Fortescue J. Tynte.[50] Fortescue Tynte's own wife died in 1899. McGee mentioned her good works on behalf of the poor and noted that her death was a great blow to the parish. The death of another member of the Tynte family led to more memorial work being carried out in the church, which was closed for some weeks in 1899 to allow three stained glass windows to be inserted to the memory of Lady Tynte. The windows were made by Heaton, Butler and Bayne of London and placed in the chancel by Col. Tynte. The parishioners also wished to have a memorial to Lady Tynte from themselves, so the nave was tiled in her memory, as 'she had endeared herself to every one of them, rich and poor alike, by her kindly interest in everything that in any way could tend towards their happiness and welfare'.[51]

As with Donovan's diary, McGee's *Retrospect* is written from a particular standpoint. Caution must be advised when the rector makes a sweeping statement claiming to speak for both the rich and the poor. Once again, no deliberate bias may be intended by the writer, but McGee's own background was upper class, and he was certainly well used to moving in landlord circles, as his description of one event in 1897 demonstrates:

> In the afternoon Colonel and Mrs. Tynte held a reception at Tynte Park, at which a large number of the surrounding gentry as well as the immediate parishioners were present. Tea was provided in a marquee in front of the house. During the afternoon a military band discoursed sweet music, and Tynte park looked its gayest, the natural beauty of itself and the magnificent view of the Wicklow mountains being enhanced by the presence of a fashionable gathering.[52]

Despite such relaxing breaks, however there is no doubt that the period 1894–99 was one of intense activity in the parish. A huge job was done on the rectory and the church was transformed during those years. A later writer commented

> It would be impossible to overestimate the debt owed by the present generation to Rev. S. R. McGee and the parishioners of his day. The church as we know it today is largely a monument to their industry ... symbolic of a religious tradition stretching back through the centuries.'[53]

That religious tradition was not neglected in the late nineteenth century. While the Church of Ireland may not have gone through the 'devotional revolution' experienced by the Catholic Church, worship was still an important element of church life. In 1894 there were three services in the church every Sunday and Holy Communion was administered twice every month. The secretary of the vestry R. G. Dixon of Milltown and the churchwardens H. F. Lawrenson M.D. and Thomas Molyneaux J.P. were engaged in carrying out the work of the parish and the average Sunday morning congregation was 140.[54] This figure was, however, only 13 per cent of the Protestant population of the parish in 1891, a much lower proportion than the Catholic attendance. Religious practice in the Protestant parish was further enhanced by the Mutual Improvement Association, which was open to both men and women 'on terms of equality'. Meetings of the association opened with a prayer, after which there was a bible study session. Once the religious aspect of the evening was over, one of the members would read a paper to the meeting. These papers were very varied with 'Domestic Animals', 'Foretelling the Weather' and 'Ladies Dress' being three examples of topics chosen.[55] The Mutual Improvement Association contributed to the sense of 'order, decency, beauty and dignity' referred to by Plunket on the occasion of his visit to Dunlavin in 1895.

In 1901 Archbishop Peacocke was in Dunlavin to dedicate a new church organ. On 20 February 1901 Peacocke impressed the necessity of devotional worship on his Dunlavin congregation. He also said that sacred music was helpful to worship and noted that the new organ completed the work that had been in execution at intervals over the past seven years.[56] McGee was the guiding spirit behind the work in the parish at the time, but he was at pains to point to the work of others in his *Retrospect*. Tynte, Pennefather and Dixon of Milltown were all obvious upper class candidates for McGee's thanks, but he also mentioned Mr. W. Couse, 'a real old soldier, an Indian mutiny man, loved and respected by everyone'. Two teachers also merited special mention, Mr. Giltrap of Tynte Park school, 'one of the old church education teachers' and J. A. Douglas of Dunlavin school before he went to Balbriggan. 'Such men' McGee wrote 'in their various ways did much to develop an atmosphere of quiet dignity, which was an outstanding feature of the people of the district reaching from Dunlavin right into the Glen of Imaal'. McGee included Dunlavin and the Glen of Imaal in the same region despite noting the psychological division of the people elsewhere in his *Retrospect*.[57]

McGee remained in Dunlavin until 1905. His *Retrospect* was published in 1935 and he called it a 'record of a period in the parochial life of Dunlavin.'[58] This is indeed the case, but most of the allusions and anecdotes in the booklet concern the Unionist upper class in Dunlavin. McGee was a staunch Unionist and three of his abiding memories of his time in Dunlavin were the visit of his Royal Highness the duke of Connaught; the visits paid by Princess Margaret and Princess Patricia to the town, which led him to comment on the charming characteristics of each member of the Royal family; and bringing forty young people from Dunlavin to see Queen Victoria when she visited Dublin in April 1900, after which the children had tea, buns and oranges in the R.I.C. depot in the Phoenix Park before returning to Dunlavin by train.[59] In fact, the booklet written by the upper class Unionist McGee is in many ways the perfect foil to the diary kept by the middle class nationalist Donovan. Both record aspects of parish life in Dunlavin during the late nineteenth century. They deal with different religious traditions, but more importantly, they work at different levels. The experiences of the two pastors and of their communities were quite different during this period. The question of socio-political control was central to these differences. Gladstone's Disestablishment Act was the start of a slippery slope for the Protestant establishment in Dunlavin, and this led to a power struggle, with some sectarian undertones, in local politics during this period. The next chapter will examine this phenomenon in more detail.

Donovan's politics: nationalist Dunlavin, 1881–1901

The latter years of the nineteenth century were dominated by a struggle for social and political control in the Dunlavin area. In 1881, despite Gladstone's second land act, the position of landlords, including Dunlavin's principal landlord Joseph Pratt-Tynte, seemed assured. By 1901, however, this was no longer the case. Local politics was by then dominated by nationalists, not Unionists, and the burning issue at the heart of the power struggle was land. This chapter will examine how the struggle for political and agrarian control impacted at local level in and around Dunlavin in Fr. Donovan's time.

The Dunlavin area was one where tenant grievances regarding landlord policy had existed for many years. At the start of the nineteenth century William Ryves had evicted almost all Catholic tenants from his lands around Rathsallagh in the aftermath of the 1798 Rebellion.[1] Only one Catholic family, the Nortons, survived these evictions.[2] The head of this family, John Norton, gave evidence before the Devon Commission in 1845. He lived on a 102 acre farm on Edward Pennefather's land in Rathsallagh, but he also held two other farms, bringing the total area farmed by him to 'near 500 acres.'[3] Arrears of rent were sometimes dealt with by putting the debtors' cattle in the pound, but 'the usual mode of recovering rent was by ejectment.'[4] Tenants leasing from a middleman were worse off than those leasing under the head landlord because 'the middleman will press for the rent.'[5] Any improvements made to holdings were carried out by tenants, not landlords, who, according to Norton's evidence, 'in general do not give anything – they do not give as much as a slate' if improvements were being carried out.[6] Landlords in the area made no allowance 'for draining or any other agricultural improvement.'[7] Some consolidation of smaller farms had been effected, especially on Lord Wicklow's property situated in the Glen of Imaal, but the method of consolidation involved evicting smaller tenant farmers.[8] These evictions in the Glen had a sectarian element to them as 'Catholics were pushed up the mountainside, while Protestant families were brought into the better lands below.'[9] Fr. Shearman had noted in 1862 that around Dunlavin 'Catholics in general with a few exceptions aren't wealthy.'[10] John Norton of Rathsallagh, holding nearly 500 acres in three farms, was obviously one such exception. Despite the dismal situation for tenant farmers described by Norton, his own wealth ensured that he was one of the leading Catholic farmers in the

Dunlavin region during the latter years of the nineteenth century.[11] John Norton's son Joseph was a personal friend of Parnell,[12] and a leading member of the Dunlavin branch of the Land League, which was the first branch to be established in County Wicklow.[13] The nationalist *Leinster Leader* referred to him in 1898 as 'Joe Norton of Rathsallagh, a thorough Irish gentleman of the old school . . . a veteran of Land League days.'[14] The Land League was formed on 21 October 1879, with a County Wicklow landlord, Charles Stewart Parnell as its president.[15] The real genesis of the League may be traced to the Irishtown meeting of March 1879, which was 'a great success,'[16] and the movement spread rapidly. On 21 November 1880 branches of the Land League were established in Dunlavin and Baltinglass.[17] Both towns are in west Wicklow and it was not surprising that these were the first branches of the League in county Wicklow as 'relationships with landlords were more fraught in the less prosperous west of the county.'[18]

In 1881 the Bessborough Commission published its findings regarding the working of the 1870 land act and the general state of land holding in Ireland. The commission interviewed no witness from Dunlavin, but three witnesses from neighbouring parishes did give evidence. These were Thomas Robertson of Narraghmore, John La Touche of Harristown and Edward Fenlon of Kilcullen.[19] These accounts from neighbouring parishes reflected the situation around Dunlavin also – Fenlon claimed to 'represent the feelings of the vast majority of the farmers of Kildare and neighbouring Wicklow.'[20] All three witnesses told similar stories – large increases in rent were common, but the tenants lacked any form of security as the 'Ulster custom' did not exist in the area.[21] Landlords in the area still did not make any allowances for improvements carried out by tenants. John Norton had commented on this to the Devon Commission in 1845, and all three witnesses to the Bessborough Commission confirmed that this had not changed by 1881. La Touche, a landlord himself, saw no reason why the tenant should have any claims for improvements,[22] but Robertson and Fenlon saw the question of tenant improvements not being recognised as very unfair.[23]

The unfair system of Irish landholding was tackled by Gladstone's second land act of August 1881. However, many Land Leaguers thought that the act did not go far enough and did not accept it. Some members were arrested for obstructing the act. These included John Dowling and Philip Healy of the Dunlavin branch and E. P. O'Kelly, George O'Toole and John Power of the Baltinglass branch, all of whom were imprisoned in October 1881.[24] These arrests suggest agrarian unrest in west Wicklow, but the Kilmainham Treaty of April 1882 calmed the situation and disbanded the Land League in one fell swoop. However, support for Land Leaguers remained strong in the Dunlavin area. When Mr. Byrne of Baltinglass was released from Naas gaol on 1 April 1883, where he had been imprisoned on a charge of boycotting, he returned to Baltinglass via Dunlavin 'where he got a very cordial reception and fifty carloads of supporters waited to accompany him to Baltinglass. The Crehelp brass band gave a stirring selection of music and Mr. Byrne's procession assumed immense proportions as it left Dunlavin for Baltinglass'.[25]

The Irish National League was founded on 17 October 1882 'to attain the following objects: (1) national self-government, (2) land law reform, (3) local self-government, (4) extension of franchises and (5) encouragement of Irish labour and industrial interests'.[26] Land reform was now relegated to the status of a secondary objective, while home rule was the primary objective of the new organisation, thus marking a transition from social to political agitation. This transition however was not always apparent at local level in National League branches.[27] It may have been the case at national level, but at local level National League meetings were dominated by the land question and it was the stronger farmers who held control of the organisation.[28] Perhaps the reality was that gaining home rule was equated to gaining control of the land by the members of the National League in Dunlavin in the 1880s. The Dunlavin branch of the National League had its origins in a meeting held on Dunlavin green on Sunday 22 July 1883. A large crowd assembled on the fairgreen and bands from Crehelp, Donard, Ballymore-Eustace and Crookstown raised the spirits of the crowd. The meeting began at 3.30 p.m., but the crowd had been at fever pitch since the arrival of T. D. Sullivan and Denis Moran from Dublin at 1 p.m. Moran was a poor law guardian from Dublin, but Sullivan was a leading Parnellite and editor of *The Nation*, who had become an M.P. for Westmeath in 1880.[29] Sullivan's presence on the platform meant that this was an important meeting and ensured a very large attendance. The shorthand writer who took notes on the proceedings was under police protection. Sullivan's address did not disappoint the crowd. Sullivan began his speech by referring to the massacre on Dunlavin green in 1798: 'It's not the first time that this historic green of Dunlavin saw men ready to stand and suffer for the holy cause of Ireland. It has been consecrated by the heart's blood of Irish patriots and this generation of Dunlaviners is as ready as their fathers to do their duty by Ireland. The men of '98 did not fall in vain'. Sullivan then went on to denounce the landlord system

> It was impossible for Ireland to thrive, to have security in your own homesteads or to enjoy the rewards of your own industry, but we arose and we have maimed the evil. We have broken the back of Irish landlordism and all the doctors in the British empire cannot repair it. Our banner is 'The land for the people' and under that banner we will fight and conquer.

While the National League relegated land reform to the status of a secondary objective behind home rule, Sullivan's speech in Dunlavin definitely concentrated on land reform. This theme would have struck a chord with the attendance of the meeting, which was chaired by E. P. Kelly, the ex-Land

League agitator from Baltinglass. O'Kelly expressed three aims in his address; to obtain another, more just, land act, to seek a better deal for the agricultural labourers and to ensure that never again would a Whig or Tory represent Wicklow in parliament. The order of O'Kelly's aims again suggests that land reform was seen as a more important priority than home rule at local level, despite the official National League position.

Sullivan ended his speech with a plea

> I ask you then to form in this town a Dunlavin branch of the National League. I ask you to put local differences and jealousies aside for the sake of Ireland . . . There is room for improvement in this town, there ought to be a flourishing branch of the Irish National League in it and I hope that very soon there will be one.

This message was well received by his audience which included many nationalist strong farmers. J. Harrington, Joseph Norton, Terence Higgins, Patrick Byrne, John Hayden, Martin Kavanagh, Thomas Metcalfe, Michael Healy, Thomas McDonald, Mathew Headon, Philip Healy, William Keogh and H. J. Mullally were all present. Each of these families figured as prominent occupiers of land in 1854.[30] Land and landholding were vital in late nineteenth-century rural Ireland, and these strong farming families had held on to what they had, so there was a high degree of continuity in strong farming circles during the thirty years between Griffith's valuation and the meeting on Dunlavin green in 1883. H. J. Mullally, a nationalist farmer who lived in Lemonstown, addressed the meeting and reminded all present of the plight of 'two poor men in Friar Hill who do not know the day they are to be evicted. One of them lives in a roofless cabin and is in rapid consumption, but he and the other man are about being turned out by the crowbar brigade.' Mullally encouraged all present to 'stand together under the banner of the National League to prevent such happenings.' Yet again the wording of Mullally's address indicated that the National League was seen as an instrument of land reform rather than of home rule at grassroots level in the Dunlavin area.

The Dunlavin green meeting of 22 July 1883 passed three resolutions, once again putting land reform as the first priority. These resolutions were

> (1) to use every legitimate means to have the land act's many defects amended, (2) to strengthen the local branches of the National League and to establish a branch in Dunlavin and (3) To agitate to have the agricultural labourer placed in a position to clothe himself and his family and procure a suitable education for his children.

The plight of the agricultural labourer was urgent, but it was very definitely last on the list of resolutions passed by the meeting, even though E. P. O'Kelly asked all present 'to unite in the cause of both farmer and labourer. The question of the labourers is a big one and hard to deal with, but there is a good day coming.'[31] O'Kelly's optimism was groundless though, and he seemed to be including the labourers for the sake of saying the right thing – even if it was only lip service. The underclass remained! T. D. Sullivan left Dunlavin for Sallins station amid music from the bands. The railway did not reach Dunlavin till 1885, and the Tullow branch was only in the planning stages at this time. It would be two more years before the plans became a reality under engineer Robert Worthington.[32] Sullivan promised to carry the word to the central branch of the National League that 'they may depend on the County Wicklow and the men of the town of Dunlavin.'[33]

The Dunlavin branch of the National League was up and running by the time that Frederick Donovan became parish priest of Dunlavin on 17 April 1884.[34] The League flourished during 1884 and in June of that year it was decided to incorporate Donard as well. This decision was taken at a meeting held on 29 June at the committee rooms of the Dunlavin National League in Tornant. Thomas Norton chaired the meeting. The Norton family had occupied nearly 213 acres in Tornant since the 1850s, subletting to Michael Byrne and Michael Somers.[35] They were one of the strongest nationalist farming families in the district and Thomas Norton's position of chairman of the Dunlavin branch of the National League reflected this. Many other strong farmers were also present at the Tornant meeting including Michael Healy, James Kelly, James Cunningham, Joseph Norton, Thomas Byrne, William Keogh, Matthew Headon, Thomas Metcalfe and Thomas Moody. Others present included Thomas O'Toole, Patrick Costello and Capt. W. Cassidy. It is significant that this list includes many strong farmers, but local shopkeepers are not mentioned at all. Names of prominent merchants like Edward Fay, Martin Kelly and J. Harrington (Tynte Arms) are conspicuous by their absence, indicating that the larger farmers controlled the local branch of the National League. Two resolutions were passed at the meeting on 29 June (1) That the books for enrolling members be closed on 31 August and that no subscriptions be paid except to the duly appointed collectors. (proposer: Thomas Metcalfe, Oldmill; seconder: Michael Healy, Tober) and (2) that a meeting be held at Mr. Thomas Metcalfe's, Oldmill, near Donard on Sunday 20 July to enrol new members for Donard and Davidstown districts. (proposer: Thomas McDonald, Lemonstown; seconder: Matthew Headon, Tornant).[36]

The meeting at Oldmill on 20 July was attended by nearly 1,000 people. The Donard and Crehelp brass bands were both present. Thomas Norton again took the chair and the list of those present included the usual strong farming families, along with many strong farmers from the Donard area, including the Allen, Brien, Murphy, Tyrrell and Whittle families (all of whom are listed in *Slater's Directory* for 1881). The speeches were ultra-nationalistic. Reference was made to the fact that this area was home to 'Michael Dwyer of historic Imaal'. Parnell was compared to Tone, Emmet, Fitzgerald, Smith O'Brien, Davis and Kickham. Indeed, judging by the tone of Norton's speech, there was a very fine line indeed between the National League's aspirations to home rule and the Fenians' aspirations to complete independence! Once more the land question figured prominently with the speakers. Norton told the assembly 'Scarcely a day passes without some heartless evictions. Let your battle cry be 'The land of Ireland for the people of Ireland'.[37] Again, the National League was perceived as an instrument of land reform at grass roots level. This is why the organisation was so attractive to the strong farmers, who obviously dominated the movement in the Dunlavin area.

The National League was only one arena in the overall power struggle that was taking place during these decades. Thomas Norton instructed all League members to pay their rates by 1 July 1884 'so as not to lose their votes.'[38] Despite this, in March 1885, when Anthony Metcalfe of Lemonstown stood for election as poor law guardian in the Dunlavin division of the Baltinglass Union, he was defeated by the sitting Conservative guardian, Richard Fisher of Merginstown by ninety-five votes to sixty-six. Canon Donovan attributed this 'minority of 29' to 'landlord multiple votes' and, although disappointed with the result, he took heart from the fact that this poor law guardian contest for the Dunlavin division was the first on record and a sign of changing times. At national level, County Wicklow was represented in parliament by W. J. Corbet. Corbet had not been present with T. D. Sullivan at the Dunlavin green meeting of 22 July 1883, but a letter conveying his apologies and supporting Sullivan had been read out.[39] When the nationalists of County Wicklow resolved to present Corbet 'their faithful representative in parliament with an address and presentation' Donovan sanctioned a church gate collection for the purpose. The collection held on 19 July 1885 amounted to £34 7s. 10d. When compared to other collections, this figure is high. The diocesan educational fund in October 1884 had only come to £14. 14s., while even the Peter's Pence collection for Pope Leo XIII in July 1884 (traditionally a 'silver collection') had only amounted to £23. 5s. Donovan undoubtedly exhorted his congregation to give generously to any nationalist collection, thus contributing to the flourishing state of the National League in Dunlavin, and of the wider Home Rule party in general.

The year 1885 was also an election year. This election was the first to operate under the newly enlarged franchise. The £12 valuation threshold had been abolished and Donovan was pleased that Gladstone had taken this step as well as 'disestablished an alien church, passed townland acts and endeavoured to pass an education bill'. But Gladstone's ballot act was, Donovan thought, 'the most useful of all. Not long since, bodies of tenants would be swept along to the poll by agents and bailiffs who knew how they would vote, and were surrounded by troops of infantry and horse and driven to the hustings like slaves, and if they refused to go they were marked men.' Donovan rejoiced that now 'every voter can vote for whom he likes, every household has a vote under certain conditions, every cabinholder can have as good a vote and a right to vote as his landlord.' Donovan foresaw that 'as a rule the landholders of the county, the shopkeepers in the towns and the labourers in their cabins will come forward in great numbers and support the choice of Mr. Parnell'.

As a result of the enlarged franchise west Wicklow was to have its own representative. The contest was between Garret Michael Byrne (Nationalist) and W. W. F. Hume Dick (Conservative), while W. J. Corbet stood against the Conservative Colonel Tottenham in the east of the county. On 22 November 1885, Fr. Donovan chaired a 'large and enthusiastic meeting' at Tornant Moat 'within a few yards of St. Nicholas's well and of the grave of the 36 martyrs who were shot down by English soldiers on Dunlavin green in 1798.' Donovan stated that he was proud to preside at this meeting organised by the Dunlavin and Donard branch of the National League. If every branch had such numbers as this 'the cause of Ireland would be gained in a short time.' Donovan had no desire to preside at public meetings but he did so on that day for the first time, as it was 'gratifying to the people and useful to the cause of their common country.' After Donovan's speech, Rev. Thomas Lynch, Donovan's curate in Donard also addressed the meeting, urging the assembly to vote for Garret Byrne so that he would be returned with 'such a majority as will prevent any other individual not in accordance with the principles of Mr. Parnell from showing his nose anytime again in west Wicklow.' Anthony Metcalfe was also among the speakers. He urged the labourers, who had the franchise for the first time, to vote for Byrne. Landlords in Baltinglass poor law union 'were doing everything in their power to obstruct the labourer's act'. Labourers were urged to 'be honest to yourselves and your families and vote for Mr. Garret Byrne, the chosen of Mr. Parnell.' The labourers duly obliged and in December 1885 Byrne defeated Hume Dick by 3,721 votes to 871, while in east Wicklow Corbet defeated Tottenham by 3,385 votes to 1,000. Donovan, delighted by the result, recorded that 'the people voted with great spirit and enthusiasm.'

One interesting aspect of the meeting at Tornant chaired by Donovan was the presence of many local shopkeepers as well as the usual quota of strong farmers. J. Harrington (Tynte Arms), Edward Fay and Martin Kelly were all present, indicating that many of the Catholic mercantile community of Dunlavin were nationalist and pro-home rule in their outlook, even though they were not involved in the local branch of the National League. They probably saw the League as being primarily oriented towards land reform, which was not an issue that concerned shopkeepers. The usual farmers were of course also present at Tornant Moat – Thomas Metcalfe for example – as well as E.P. O'Kelly from Baltinglass, 'ex-suspect', and P.J. Whelan 'representative of the labourers.'[40]

In March 1886 the office of poor law guardian for Rathsallagh division was contested between W. Bolton (Conservative) and Joseph Norton (Nationalist).

Norton won by a narrow margin, sixty-three votes to sixty-one. Donovan was ecstatic about Norton's victory. This was the first time that a Catholic had represented Rathsallagh division and Donovan recorded that Norton's election was a milestone that happened because of a 'well planned and well fought contest' by the nationalists in Rathsallagh. Nationalist planning and organisational skills were needed again in July when Gladstone dissolved parliament 'that the constituencies might vote whether Ireland was to be granted Home Rule.' West Wicklow was again contested and Donovan took delight in recording that on 12 July there were 3,531 votes for Garret Byrne against 856 for W. Hume Dick, 'a Parnellite majority of 2,675.'

After this election, Parnell and his party were at the height of their powers, but in March 1887 the *Times* attacked Parnell and his followers in its articles 'Parnellism and crime.' These Pigott forgeries led to a commission of enquiry which operated during 1888 and 1889. In October 1888, Donovan sanctioned a collection for 'the national indemnity fund, towards the expenses of the judicial commission regarding Parnell and the other Irish M.P.s.' Once again, Donovan exhorted the people to give generously and 'the Dunlavin parochial contribution amounted to the sum of £40.' This figure may be put into context by comparing it to the July 1888 Peter's pence 'silver collection' which amounted to £18 12s.[41]

Despite the high profile of the Irish Party, the land question was still a burning issue at local level. One case before Joseph Pratt-Tynte and William Heighington at Dunlavin petty sessions on Wednesday, 25 July 1888 involved an evicted tenant, Mrs. Brady. She was charged with taking forcible possession of the premises from which she was evicted by George Farrell of Ballymore-Eustace. Mrs. Brady had returned to the house and occupied a pigsty, from which Farrell again evicted her. At the time of the court case, the Brady family was living under the arch of Lemonstown bridge, and had their furniture there. The bench decided that justice would be served if Mrs. Brady did not return to Farrell's house, a condition to which her husband agreed and so she was discharged.[42] Evictions were an ongoing problem in the local area and in December 1889 Donovan recorded that a massive £78 3s. had been collected in Dunlavin 'for the Irish Tenants' Defence Fund.' This is the largest figure subscribed to any collection recorded in Donovan's diary, and it is obvious that Catholic Dunlaviners supported the evicted tenants, and, by implication, were behind reform of the land system. The threat to the rural establishment, embodied in Dunlavin by people such as Joseph Pratt-Tynte and Edward Pennefather, was increasing. Such developments led to some sectarian incidents in the parish, the most notable of which was the 'outrage on Donard church' in August 1888. Garret Byrne asked a question in the House of Commons 'whether it was a fact that the Roman Catholic church at Donard, County Wicklow, was some days ago decorated with Orange lilies, the doors chalked with Orange texts and the chapel bell rung, all in the dead of night . . . and whether any steps are being taken to bring the perpetrators to justice?' In reply the chief secretary said that Orange emblems were hung in the church and the bell was rung, but no texts were chalked on the door. The police had the matter under investigation.[43]

The incident at Donard church resulted in a meeting in Donard on 5 August 1888 which was attended by more than 3,000 people. Donovan, who was parish priest, did not attend the meeting. He was based in 'lowland' Dunlavin, and it was 'upland' Donard church which had been violated, so he was quite content to let his Donard curate, Patrick Brennan take the platform, even though the young Brennan had been only newly ordained from Maynooth when he replaced Thomas Lynch in June 1887. In the event, Brennan did not disappoint his audience, which included large contingents from Baltinglass, Hollywood, Blessington, Ballymore-Eustace, the Glen of Imaal and Dunlavin. Before the meeting started the grand master of Donoghmore Loyal Orange Lodge 1798, Rev. Timothy Clifford O'Connor, mounted the podium and tried to speak but he was shouted down and 'put off the platform by a man called Hurley.' There had been an Orange lodge in the Donard area for about ninety years, and generally the Orangemen were tolerated locally, but the crowd at the meeting was obviously not in a tolerant mood![44] When the chairman John Magrath of Castleruddery called on Fr. Brennan to speak, the curate delivered a fiery address. He was, he said 'sent to Donard by our holy and patriotic archbishop, Dr. Walsh, to aid his flock, save their souls and defend the honour of God's house.' Brennan would not tolerate the outrage, and went on to say that he had 'never interfered in politics, but he would put his foot down to stamp out Orangeism.' The next speaker was none other than poor law guardian E. P. O'Kelly from Baltinglass. He was even less tolerant than Brennan: 'Orangemen had too much toleration in Donard. There, on 12 July, they assembled, and brought out all their old shanderadans and decorated their old horses, their mules, their asses, their old wives and mothers and ugly orange coloured daughters – there wasn't a good looking girl among them – wait until 12 July and he would see if they have their peaceable nonsensical display unmolested.'

In spite of this threat and other anti-Orange speeches delivered by the next speakers, Mr. D. Fay, poor law guardian and Mr. H. J. Mullally of Lemonstown, there is no record of any violence in Donard on the following 12 July. Despite local Orange gestures, the nationalist tide continued to rise. In March 1889, Edward Fay, the Dunlavin merchant, was returned as poor law guardian for the Dunlavin electoral division of Baltinglass union. Fay was the first Catholic to represent Dunlavin in this position, and even though he lost his seat on the board to the Conservative Thomas Molyneux the following March, Donovan had no doubt that Fay's breakthrough was a significant one for the nationalists of Dunlavin.

All was not well within the Dunlavin branch of the National League however. In fact, by 1890 the branch was defunct. The League was not involved in the case of the Brady eviction in July 1888, so it is possible that the demise of the branch happened even earlier than 1890. On 1 February 1890, however, the *Leinster Leader* carried an article on Edward Sweetman, who was 'among the best of the Kildare landlords', but who charged John Harrington of Dunlavin a rent of £490 a year on a property which the Kane sub-commission had now valued at £340 fair rent. This sub-commission, headed by Mr. R. R. Kane, was an organ of the land commission which had been established under the 1881 land act, but whose power and scope were extended under the 1885 Ashbourne land act. The purpose of the Kane sub-commission was to hear appeals made by tenants and establish fair rents on properties. On 25 January 1890 the sub-commission met in Blessington to fix fair rents in Baltinglass union, and Harrington's appeal was one of twenty-two on which Mr. R. R. Kane delivered judgement that day. The twenty-two appeals, taken against seven landlords including Sweetman, all resulted in a rent reduction. What made the Harrington-Sweetman case significant was the scale of the reduction. The average rent reviewed was £62 11s. 6d. and the average reduction was 24.7 per cent. Harrington's rent of £490 was more than twice as much as the second largest figure, £202, and was reduced by 32 per cent. This reduction of £150 a year was very substantial and the *Leinster Leader* remarked that such a sum would be taken by many people to provide a good living for the year. Such a sum, said the article, was considerable – too considerable to be overlooked – and the *Leader* wondered if Harrington would be reimbursed by £150 a year, and if so, would it be backdated! The same issue of the newspaper however, delivered a vitriolic attack on 'the absence of a branch of the National League, or of any organisation in the parish of Dunlavin'. 'No effort' the article stated 'was being made to collect the tenants' defence fund in Dunlavin parish.' It went on ' Surely some of the people there should do something for the tenant farmers. Those who obtain reductions of £150 a year by means of the organisation should not grudge a small share of their wealth or spare a little trouble, self-interest if they are dead to gratitude ought to move them'.[45]

This broadside from the *Leinster Leader* was too much for Donovan. He wrote a scathing reply, which appeared in the paper on the following Saturday. The author of last week's article, Donovan stated, 'wrote hastily and incorrectly and pictured quite an unreal state of affairs.' If nothing was being done in Dunlavin, wrote Donovan 'it is because it has been done long since. Dunlavin was the first parish in the County Wicklow to forward its large and generous contribution of over £78 for the tenants' defence fund early last December.' Donovan was also quick to defend John Harrington, who had been alluded to in the article of the preceding week. 'The gentleman in question' stated Donovan's letter 'in the opinion of those who know him best, is not in the habit of grudging either small or large sums as circumstances may require, and on this occasion his contribution amounted to near £6.'[46] Donovan's spirited reply was only papering over the cracks however, and could not hide the fact that the Dunlavin and Donard branch of the National League was no longer in existence. Later that year the *Leinster Leader* again mentioned the fact: 'Where are the Leagues of west Wicklow? The branches in Dunlavin and Baltinglass have become extinct.'[47] H. J. Mullally, speaking at a meeting in Hollywood on 20 July 1890 said

> It was always a source of regret and pain to him that there was now no branch of the National League in his own parish of Dunlavin, he had been the first to start the land league in west Wicklow and Dunlavin was the first branch in the county, but circumstances which he could not control caused a falling off in the branch which he had established and for which he so long felt a pride, but its efficiency and work died out.

He promised 'that he would do his best to revive the organisation in Dunlavin, and if there was not a branch in full working order there within a short time, the fault would not be his!'[48] Despite Mullally's pledge, there is no record of a revival of the National League in Dunlavin in either Canon Donovan's diary or in issues of the *Leinster Leader* from the early 1890s.[49]

The reason or reasons behind the demise of the Dunlavin branch of the National League during the late 1880s must remain in the realms of conjecture. Canon Donovan's diary reveals him to have been among the most ardent supporters of the League in the early and mid 1880s, but Donovan studiously ignored any reference to the League after 1886. Similarly, all reports in the *Leinster Leader* from Dunlavin branch cease about the same time. The indications are that the League folded due to an internal feud of some kind. If this were indeed the case, it is possible that the *Leader*, a nationalist newspaper did not wish to print the details of such a disagreement. A similar argument could be applied to the *Freeman's Journal*, where there appears to be no clue either. The local Unionist newspaper, the *Kildare Observer*, probably was not privy to the details of any internal National League feud and so could not (and did not) print the story. At the seminal meeting of Dunlavin National League on Dunlavin green on 22 July 1883, T. D. Sullivan had asked all present 'to put local differences and jealousies aside for the sake of Ireland, let the spirit of brotherhood prevail. There is room for improvement in this town.' This indicated that there were tensions within the local strong farming community even before the establishment of the Dunlavin branch of the League. H. J. Mullally, a local strong farmer from Lemonstown actually told the meeting 'I know I have enemies, but so has Parnell.' Mullally's statement on 22 July 1883 may have referred to covert enemies within the local nationalist farming community.[50] If this were so, Sullivan's plea for brotherhood fell on deaf ears and the Dunlavin branch of the National League was rent asunder by its own members during the late 1880s, and reported dead by the *Leinster Leader* in 1890!

However, although the year 1890 saw the death throes of Dunlavin National League, it also witnessed the birth pangs of Dunlavin G.A.A. club. The club was founded under the name of 'Sons of St. Nicholas' at a meeting held on the 20 January 1890.[51] Donovan's curate, Rev. Francis McEnerney was the club's first president. Perhaps Donovan, who was now nearly sixty years of age, was content to leave the presidency of this athletic association to the younger man. The other officers of the club were the poor law guardian Edward Fay – vice president, Chris Lawlor – treasurer, John Rochford – secretary, Joseph Whittle – captain, Thomas Roche – vice captain. It is obvious from this list that, unlike the National League, the G.A.A was not dominated by strong farmers. Fay was, as already noted, a leading Dunlavin shopkeeper. The Whittle family were among the nine leading Catholic merchant families in Dunlavin in the 1860s.[52] Neither Rochfords nor Roches were listed among the leading local farmers in the 1880s. Chris Lawlor worked in a local public house.[53] The G.A.A. may have been a nationalistic organisation, but it was not an instrument of land reform and so the strong farming families did not seek control of the club.

The G.A.A. club played in a field which Mr. J. Norton had granted them permission to use.[54] They contested their first championship match against Baltinglass on 14 May 1890, but were defeated.[55] The championship in County Wicklow reflected the east-west divide within the county. Nearly all of the teams competing were from the west, so Bray Emmets got a bye into the finals as they were 'in a remote part of the county.'[56] Despite defeat in the championship, the Dunlavin club continued to flourish and later in 1890 held its first tournament. Any doubts about the nationalistic aspirations of the G.A.A. were soon dispelled when one saw the names of the competing teams including Irish Brigade (Ballymore-Eustace), Michael Davitts (Athgarvan) and McAllisters (Kilbaylet).[57] The G.A.A. was another element in the rising tide of nationalism in Dunlavin during the late nineteenth century, demonstrated by the success of Byrne at the polls in west Wicklow and of Fay at the polls within Baltinglass union. The link between the G.A.A. and the newly resurgent Catholicism, exemplified in Dunlavin by Fr. Donovan's work, was personified in the patronage of Archbishop Croke. In March 1890 Croke made a speech about the virtue of temperance and advocated that all G.A.A. members should take the pledge. All games in Wicklow were cancelled for one day to allow the players to do so. The proposal passed by the Dunlavin branch of the G.A.A. stated 'That we cordially respond to the pious and patriotic appeal which our Most Rev. patron had addressed to the manhood of Ireland calling on them to wipe away the one stain that disfigures the fair fame of their motherland today.'[58] The motion was proposed by Patrick Kenny and seconded by Patrick Doyle. The club obviously saw temperance as a serious issue!

Just when Dunlavin G.A.A. was developing into a major local force however came 'the unfortunate Parnell split. Nowhere was the bitterness and reaction felt so heavily and destructively as in his native county; there was little or no involvement by Dunlavin G.A.A. club over this period.'[59] Fr. Donovan was dismayed by the Parnell scandal, but he adopted an anti-Parnellite stance, which was also the official position of the Irish Catholic Church on the matter. Donovan wrote in his diary

> During this twelvemonth all Ireland was torn by dissentions, arising out of the Parnell divorce case, between two rival parties; one headed by the deposed Chief himself . . . and his numerous and noisy following, and the other consisting of the majority of the parliamentary representatives supported by the Irish hierarchy, and the bulk of the nation.

The Parnell split killed off a fledgling revival of the National League that had occurred in Donard prompted by the evictions on the Smith-Barry estate in Tipperary. A meeting had been held in Donard on 19 October 1890, chaired by Rev. J. Hickey. It was decided to send £5 to central branch to re-affiliate. Three resolutions were passed, supporting the tenants in Tipperary, supporting the actions of John Dillon and William O'Brien and condemning the role played by Balfour in the whole affair.[60] Three months later however, another meeting of the Donard National League broke up having adopted the following resolution by nineteen votes to six: 'That we, the members of the Donard branch of the Irish National League, believe Mr. Parnell, who has proved himself unfit to lead the Irish people, to be seriously imperilling the home rule cause by his present agitation.'[61] The Donard branch of the League died out again after this meeting. There was no revival of the League in Dunlavin. Some strong farmers in the area were Parnellites. These included Joe Norton of Rathsallagh and James Kelly (now poor law guardian) of Man of War, who were recruiting officers for a short-lived Parnellite organisation called the 'Army of Independence.' James Norton, Joe Norton, H. J. Mullally, J. Byrne, Peter Doyle and J. McGrath all attended the Parnell anniversary commemorations in Dublin in October 1893.[62]

The Parnell split was bitter in Dunlavin. Donovan recorded a meeting held on Dunlavin green on 14 June 1891 to establish a local branch of the Irish National Federation. This organisation replaced (or at least became a rival to) the Irish National League, which was too closely identified with Parnell himself for the anti-Parnellite camp.[63] The meeting on the green was 'very successful.' It had been intended to hold the meeting in an enclosed yard, but the crowd was too large and the venue was changed. A platform for the 'local clergy and leading representative men of the district was hastily erected by many willing hands. The union of priests and people, now sought by some to be divorced was strikingly manifested.' Donovan obviously did not see the Parnell scandal as a reason to threaten the Catholic resurgence, the local 'devotional revolution' culture or the position of parish priest. 'As the clergy addressed their flock' wrote Donovan 'their sentiments were cheered by hundreds of as good-humoured, orderly, well-disposed and faithful a people as could be found in Ireland.' The Crehelp brass band and the Inchaquire fife and drum band were in attendance. Five resolutions were passed at the meeting on the green: establishing a Dunlavin and district branch of the Irish National Federation, pledging support to the Irish parliamentary party under Mr. Justin McCarthy, stating their renewed confidence in Mr. Gladstone, calling on Mr. Parnell to release the 'Paris funds' for the benefit of evicted tenants and finally condemning the conduct of those Parnellites who, 'forgetting all sense of propriety, religion and gratitude had hissed the honoured name of that most generous, eloquent and self-sacrificing patriot, the great archbishop of Cashel at Inchicore on Sunday week.' £22 was collected for the federation fund, which included £2 contributed by Donovan himself. The one 'stain of the day' recorded by Donovan was

> a determined Parnellite counter demonstration, incited by an active personal canvass at the local fair of last week, and further urged by bilious-worded printed posters of the accepted national colour, which was convened the same day, to give the quietus to the popular Federation meeting. The result was a very peculiar gathering of ill-sorted people of a miscellaneous character. Parnellite partisans, official and otherwise, newspaper correspondents, strangers from Dublin, friends from the distance, human contributions from different parishes and counties, masters and men, parents and children, boys and girls and one jailbird recently released from incarceration, all told made up a couple of dozen, very conveniently fitting into one room.

Presumably the 'gathering of ill sorted people' included many of Donovan's National League allies from the past – men such as Norton, Kelly and Mullally for example. The language used by Donovan is very harsh, indicating just how deep the split went. Contrast Donovan's description of a 'jailbird recently released' with his proud description of E. P. Kelly as 'ex-suspect' at the Tornant meeting of 22 November 1885.

The National Federation quickly became established in Dunlavin, taking over from the defunct National League. However there was one last hurrah for the League – when James Norton, J. McGrath and Henry J. Mullally were attending the Parnell anniversary commemorations in October 1893, they described themselves respectively as president, vice president, and secretary of the Dunlavin branch of the Irish National League.[64] This did not indicate that the League enjoyed a revival in Dunlavin though. These men had held the same offices in the Dunlavin branch before its mysterious demise, and there is no indication anywhere else that the National League held meetings or transacted any business in Dunlavin in the 1890s. The descriptions of themselves given by the old Parnellites were probably a last defiant gesture, or a nostalgic remembrance of times past. The reality was that it was the National Federation, not the National League, which embodied the mainstream nationalist opinion in Dunlavin during the 1890s.

One factor that ensured the success of the fledgling Federation in Dunlavin was Donovan's support. On 2 June 1892 Donovan noted that John Rochford and Rev. Francis McEnerney from Dunlavin had been appointed as treasurer and secretary of the election expenses fund at the county convention of the Federation which was held in Bray. Dunlavin parish topped the County Wicklow list of subscribers to this election fund, contributing £38 8s.4d. This was nearly twice as much as the £20 13s. donated by Baltinglass, the second highest parish on the list. Evidently Donovan was once again exhorting his congregation to give generously. The Federation also organised a collection for the evicted tenants' fund in 1892. Donovan noted that the total of £45 1s. collected was: 'a contribution in times of most serious depression of the patriotic people of this parish who never shirk a duty. I regret, however, I must make some exceptions. There are, in this parish as in many others, some few misguided factionists of means. Not one shilling of their money have they subscribed towards the relief of their evicted fellow farmers by whose struggle they have gained. I had hopes that the result of the last west Wicklow election would have taught these people a little political sense, but I now have despair of their return to reason. They have turned their back on all their former principles and would now wreck the national hopes because they cannot blindly lead.' Donovan again used emotive language, indicating that the Parnell split was still a very raw wound in December 1892.

Donovan also listed the names of the subscribers to the evicted tenants' fund. These names represent the anti-Parnellite majority in the parish. Among the families included were Harringtons, Copelands, Metcalfes, Mooneys, Cunninghams, McDonalds, Keoghs, Haydens, Fays, Deerings, Headons, Costelloes, Whittles, Healys, Sinotts and Lawlors. Of forty-six surnames recorded by Donovan, at least twenty-eight of them are drawn from leading farming families. This represents 61 percent of the total, indicating that the Federation was dominated by strong farmers in the Dunlavin region, just as the League had been before it. Of the other names on the list, at least five came for Dunlavin's mercantile community, but shopkeepers were obviously heavily outnumbered by farmers in the Federation's Dunlavin branch. Farming families not mentioned in Donovan's list included Nortons, Kellys, McGraths, Mullallys, Byrnes, Doyles, Barretts and Stapletons. These Parnellites were among the people who, according to Donovan 'had not been taught political sense by the result of the last west Wicklow election.'

That election was held on 13 July 1892, and was preceded by a 'great nationalist meeting on Dunlavin green on Sunday 19 June to organise for the success of Mr. James O'Connor, the selected candidate for west Wicklow at the general election. Large deputations from the neighbouring parishes attended, the parish priests of Dunlavin, Baltinglass, Ballymore-Eustace, Boystown and Eadestown and the Dunlavin curates; the Crehelp brass band and the Crookstown fife and drum band played national airs. Rev. F. A. Donovan, P.P.,V.F., Dunlavin, occupied the chair, and among the other speakers were Mr.T. J. Condon M.P. [for east Tipperary],[65] Mr. J. O'Connor and Rev. F. McEnerney C.C. Dunlavin'. This meeting on the green must have seemed like old times to Donovan who noted with satisfaction that 'much enthusiasm was displayed.' The meeting bore fruit when James O'Connor (Nationalist) was duly elected on 13 July with 2,582 votes. Col. R. P. Saunders (Conservative) polled 784 votes and J. H. Parnell (Factionist) 546. Donovan noted gleefully that the majority over Toryism was 1,798; the figure is heavily underlined in Donovan's diary; and the majority over the Parnellites was 2,030. The contest in east Wicklow had been closer. Donovan gives the figures as Sweetman (Nationalist) 1,433, Halpin (Tory) 1,225 and Corbet (Factionist) 1,115. The fact that the sitting M.P. was Parnellite had badly split the home rule vote in east Wicklow, but Donovan noted satisfactorily that two 'Nationalists' had been returned in the county. At local level, in December 1892, Donovan noted that 'Mr. Andrew Byrne was elected unopposed as coroner of west Wicklow. He was the first Catholic elected in Wicklow to this position this century. Times are much altered'. The National Federation continued to function in Dunlavin during the 1890s. In May 1894 the sum of £24 16s. 6d. was received from Dunlavin parish by the evicted tenants' fund.[66] Canon Donovan[67] noted that this was well down on the £78 3s. 6d. and the £45 1s. collected for the fund in December 1889 and December 1892 respectively, but he also noted that 'happily we have no evicted tenants here and we are only influenced by feelings of justice and humanity.' Times had changed since the late 1880s and there was obviously no case like the eviction of the Brady family of Lemonstown in 1888 to concentrate minds in Dunlavin parish in 1894. Coupled with the lack of evictions was the fact that Parnellites would not subscribe to any National Federation collection, which was another factor behind the decreasing amounts collected for the fund.

One man who still subscribed to Irish National Federation funds was John Harrington. On 5 June 1894 Donovan recorded that Harrington, a J.P. from Cannycourt had 'subscribed £10 to the Federation parliamentary fund. He is honourable and manly enough to avow his national principles and unselfish enough not to spare his purse in their support. Mere barren sympathy and lip praise do duty for patriotism with many, but fall very short of his idea of duty.' The failure of the second home rule bill in the House of Lords in 1893 did not seem to upset Donovan unduly as he continued 'We seem to be now nearing the goal of our expectation. We have a friendly government in power willing, so far as practicable, to grant our legitimate demands, our representatives may be said to live in the House of Commons for our benefit and it is our duty to support them there by our relatively cheap sacrifices'. Real sacrifices were required in February 1895 because of a 'long and continued snowstorm' resulting in much hardship in the district. Mr. Supple, the district inspector of the R.I.C. organised a charity concert 'in relief of the poor and unemployed of the district.' The star attraction at the concert which was held in the railway goods store, Dunlavin, was Mr. Percy French, 'who caused any amount of mirth.' After the concert, Donovan made a speech thanking Mr. Supple for 'so agreeable a social meeting and so successful a charity.' Despite the relief provided by the R.I.C. concert, the harsh winter may have been one factor behind the decrease in the next collection for the local Irish National Federation fund in May 1895, which only raised £21 16s. 6d. Donovan noted that this amount was collected in the parish 'notwithstanding the strain on the very limited resources of our farmers by reason of the low prices obtainable at fairs and markets and in spite of the many pecuniary sacrifices made in years past for the common good, the people of the parish continue to set a patriotic example of generosity.'

Nationalist progress continued during 1895. In March two 'pronounced nationalists' were elected as chairman and vice chairman of Baltinglass board of guardians. This was the first time that Baltinglass union had been under nationalist control. The election of the two, E. P. O'Kelly and James Coleman, Griffinstown, was undoubtedly a watershed in Baltinglass poor law union. As late as 1890, the *Leinster Leader* reported, 'The doings of the Tory deadheads who rule the roost at Baltinglass often afford interesting reading on the law as it is administered by them.'[68] The election of O'Kelly and Coleman was seen as 'an indication of the present progress of democratic power in the country.' Donovan remained optimistic about the implementation of home rule. In February 1895 he wrote: 'The success of the home rule measure is now so assured that apathy at the present juncture would be little short of criminal.' Donovan was overjoyed when E. P. O'Kelly of Baltinglass was returned as M.P. for east Wicklow at a by-election, but success was short lived and in July 1895 Donovan recorded that in the general election 'the English Liberals were completely routed and the Conservatives returned with a 152 majority. Mr. James O'Connor returned unopposed for west Wicklow, but Mr. E. P. O'Kelly now resigning and Mr. W. Corbet (Parnellite) was returned.' Obviously the Parnell split was still festering. The final entry of a political nature in Canon Donovan's diary concerns the 'unopposed election of Mr. John Germaine J.P. (Nationalist) as coroner for the west Wicklow division' and is dated 2 September 1895. Donovan died in 1896 and he left behind him a county divided between its two parliamentary representatives and a parish containing a bitter rift between its anti-Parnellite majority and its Parnellite minority. There is no suggestion here that Donovan could have prevented this, but the split was now a fact of nationalist life.

At national level it has been suggested that it was William O'Brien's United Irish League, founded in January 1898 and named for the rebels of 1798, that 'threatened the hegemony of the Irish party and enforced its reunification.'[69] In Dunlavin, one event that drew the Parnellites and anti-Parnellites closer together was the centennial commemoration of the 1798 massacre on Dunlavin green. On 29 May 1898 a large meeting was held in Dunlavin and 'the chair was taken by Mr. Thomas Metcalfe P.L.G., Crehelp, in the absence of Very Rev. Fr. Maxwell P.P.' Amongst those on the platform were members of both nationalist camps – anti-Parnellites such as James Cunningham, John Harrington and Mark Deering were joined by Parnellites including Henry J. Mullally, James Kelly junior and J. Byrne. Two leading Parnellite veterans 'absent through the hand of death, Joe Norton Rathsallagh, who had been a close personal friend of the dead Chief and James Kelly senior, the Man O'War', merited special mention. After patriotic speeches by Mr. Hugh McCarthy, Mr. G. Sweeney, Mr. J. J. Burke and 'several local speakers', the second chair was taken by the Parnellite, H. J. Mullally, who thanked the anti-Parnellite chairman, Thomas Metcalfe – an example of power sharing and a gesture of reconciliation within the Dunlavin nationalist community. That night 'the town was brilliantly illuminated. A huge bonfire blazed on the green and a torchlight procession, headed by bands proceeded to Tornant churchyard, where the martyrs sleep.'[70] This procession was described as 'a weird and impressive sight, and partook more of a religious than of a political character.'[71]

There were indications of healing within the divided nationalist community of Dunlavin as the nineteenth century drew to a close. The nationalists, who had come so far in terms of gaining political control at local level within Dunlavin district, were now drawing together once again, but the wounds would take some time to heal. After protracted negotiations the two wings of the Irish parliamentary party were reunited under chairman John Redmond in February 1900.[72] Canon Frederick Augustine Donovan P.P.,V.F., Dunlavin, would no doubt have been overjoyed, had he lived to see it happen.

Conclusion

Such, then was Dunlavin and its rural hinterland in and around the time of Canon Donovan. The object of this pamphlet has been to paint a picture of the region in the 1880s and 1890s, but more specifically to paint such a picture using Donovan's paintbrush. His diary has been central to this study and all other sources are used to flesh out the information contained on its pages. The diary leaves some questions unanswered – notably the question of why the Dunlavin branch of the Irish National League became defunct during the late 1880s. This work however is not a study of the land question in Dunlavin at this time, nor of the internal tensions within the local nationalist community. Donovan's eloquent silence raises the question of the National League's demise but it does not answer it. No doubt Donovan knew the full story behind the demise of the local National League, but he did not write about it. Perhaps he also kept out of the feud at the time.

Donovan's world revolved around the village of Dunlavin, its Roman Catholic church and his own involvement in politics. The village was a market town, serving both a west Wicklow and a Kildare hinterland. Economically it was in decline, despite some high spots like the arrival of the railway in 1885. The rate of decline had stabilised since the mid-nineteenth century however, due in part to the safety valve of out-migration from the region. Birth rates were declining too and Donovan's flock was diminishing. Despite this, devotional practice remained strong in the Roman Catholic parish. This was due in no small measure to the actions of Donovan himself. He was the local agent of the devotional revolution at this time, the broker between his flock and the pomp of the confident, resurgent Catholic church. Donovan's purchases for his churches and his improvements to the schools and parochial houses cemented his position as broker between the parish and the wider Church. His public role in the presence of Archbishop Walsh further enhanced his status. Donovan found this status very useful when he entered the arena of local politics.

Donovan was strongly nationalist and threw himself willingly into the struggles for land reform and home rule. He was a leading figure in the Dunlavin branch of the National League before its mysterious demise. No doubt Donovan supported the local G.A.A. club, but preferred to leave the active involvement in the association to his younger curate, McEnerney. However land was the burning issue within local politics. Donovan campaigned vigorously for land reform and exhorted his flock to contribute generously to any nationalist church gate collection. He was an avid supporter of Parnell, but at the time of the split he became a leading anti-Parnellite, possibly influencing the majority of his flock. He was instrumental in setting up the anti-Parnellite National Federation in Dunlavin; a village where the Parnell split was felt very deeply.

Donovan probably fell into ill health during the last year or so of his life as his diary ends on 30 September 1895. This diary provides a unique insight into the world of late nineteenth century Dunlavin. One of the most fascinating aspects of the diary is Donovan's juxtaposition of everyday parish events such as the purchase of new vestments or repairs to the schools alongside events of national significance like the election of Archbishop Walsh or the split in the wake of the Parnell divorce scandal. In this way Donovan's diary helps to place Dunlavin within the context of the wider world. Life in Dunlavin is shown as part of a wider network, yet the village and its hinterland are always central to Donovan's writings.

The Dunlavin experience perceived by Donovan may not have been unique. Dunlavin may or may not have been typical of many other villages – in so far as any place can be seen as 'typical', because every village and every community is different. Modern approaches to local history see this as a central fact. In any event, comparative studies would be needed before the 'typicality' of the Dunlavin experience of Donovan's diary could be judged. Whether typical, atypical or, as I believe, unique, Dunlavin in Donovan's time can certainly be studied through a unique primary source. Donovan's two predecessors as parish priest, Canon Hyland and Canon Whittle, are both remembered by wall-plaques in Dunlavin R.C. church. There is no memorial to Donovan in stone there, but his diary has indeed made him the 'Soggarth Aroon' to the local historian of Dunlavin.

Notes

INTRODUCTION

1 Patrick J. Corish, *The Catholic community in the seventeenth and eighteenth centuries* (Dublin, 1981) p. 2.
2 W. G. Hoskins, *Local history in England* (3rd ed., London, 1984) p. 46.
3 Dermot James and Séamas Ó Maitiú, *The Wicklow world of Elizabeth Smith 1840–1850* (Dublin, 1996).
4 The term 'devotional revolution' was first used by the historian Emmet Larkin in 1972.
5 Raymond Gillespie and Gerard Moran (eds), '*A various country' essays in Mayo history 1500–1900* (Westport, 1987) p. 12.
6 H. P. R. Finberg, *The local historian and his theme* (Leicester, 1965) p. 5.

DONOVAN'S PLACE: THE DUNLAVIN REGION, 1891–1901

1 Very Rev. Patrick O'Byrne, 'West Wicklow' in *Souvenir Guide and Programme of the Imaal Bazaar and Fete* (Naas, 1926) p. 56.
2 *The agricultural statistics for Ireland for the year 1880* [C2932], H.C. 1881, xciii, p. 30.
3 Samuel Russell McGee, *Dunlavin, Co. Wicklow – A Retrospect* (Dublin, 1935) p. 14.
4 *The agricultural statistics for Ireland for the year 1880* [C2932], H.C. 1881, xciii, p. 30.
5 *The agricultural statistics for Ireland for the year 1880* [C2932], H.C. 1881, xciii, p. 30.
6 Richard Griffith, *General valuation of rateable property in Ireland. county Wicklow, union of Baltinglass, parishes of Dunlavin and Donard.* (Dublin 1854) pp 12–26.
7 Lord Walter Fitzgerald, 'Dunlavin, Tornant and Tober, County Wicklow' in *Journal of the Co. Kildare Archaeological Society*, vii, no. 4, (1913) p. 223.
8 Trinity College Dublin, Molyneaux papers Ms. 883/2 p. 87.
9 John Lynott, 'The Bulkeley-Worth-Tynte connection' in *Dunlavin Festival of Arts Brochure* (1990) p. 59.
10 N. U. I. Maynooth, Shearman Papers, vii, f. 142v.
11 Dunlavin village was the scene of a mass execution in 1798 and Dunlavin parish saw guerrilla action until December 1803. See Chris Lawlor, *The massacre on Dunlavin Green* (Naas 1998).
12 See J. J. Lee, 'On the accuracy of the pre-famine census' in L. A. Clarkson and M. Goldstrom (eds) *Irish population, economy and society* (Oxford, 1981) pp 37–56.

13 *Census of Ireland 1821* County of Wicklow, Talbotstown Baronies, pp 128–129.
14 Claude Chavasse, *The story of Baltinglass* (Kilkenny 1970) p. 62.
15 *Correspondence for January to March 1847 relating to the measures adopted for the relief of distress in Ireland.* (Board of Works series) [C796], H.C. 1847, lii, p. 20.
16 Chris Lawlor, 'Dunlavin – foundation, famine and beyond' in *Dunlavin Festival of Arts Brochure* (1993) pp 21–22.
17 *Census of Ireland 1901*, County of Wicklow, Tables xxx and xxxviii pp 89 and 113.
18 Dunlavin R.C. Parish Registers, Volumes 1 and 2, October 1815 and October 1847, (unpaginated).
19 The Famine in Co. Wicklow, educational pack, (W.C.C. 1996), sheet 11.
20 *Slater's Directory* 1881, (London and Manchester) p. 351.
21 *Leinster Leader*, 15 March 1890.
22 *Census of Ireland 1901*, County of Wicklow, Table xxxviii p. 113.
23 M. E. Collins, *The Land Question 1879–1882* (Dublin 1974) p. 12.
24 Figures adapted from T. Barrington 'Irish Agricultural Prices' in *Journal of the statistical and social enquiry society of Ireland*, XV, pp 251–252. (See Chris Lawlor, The Wicklow World of Canon F. A. Donovan: Dunlavin 1884–1896, unpublished MA thesis, N.U.I. Maynooth) Appendix 2.
25 Tables 1 and 2 are drawn from *The agricultural statistics for Ireland* series of parliamentary papers between 1875 and 1880.
[C1568], H.C. 1876, lxxviii, p. 24.
[C1749], H.C. 1877, lxxxv, p. 28.
[C1938], H.C. 1878, lxxviii, p. 30.
[C2347], H.C. 1878–1879, lxxv, p. 30. [C2534], H.C. 1880, lxxvi, p. 32. [C2932], H.C. 1881, xciii, p. 30.
26 Figures in this section are taken from *The agricultural statistics for Ireland* series. [C1568], H.C. 1876, lxxviii, pp 34–35 and 49; [C2932], H.C. 1881, xciii, pp 40–41 and 58; [C3332], H.C. 1882, lxxiv pp 21 and 45; [C5084], H.C. 1887, lxxxix, pp 21 and 45.
27 Chris Lawlor, 'Dunlavin – foundation, famine and beyond' in *Dunlavin Festival of Arts Brochure* (1993) p. 24.
28 Chris Lawlor, 'Townland ghosts and some reflections' in *Dunlavin – Donard – Davidstown Parish Link*, iv, no. 1, (1998) p. 6.
29 Cora Crampton, 'The Tullow Line' in *Journal of the West Wicklow Historical Society*, i (1983–1984) p. 8.

30 Bar graphs compiled from census data. *Census of Ireland 1881*, County Wicklow, Table vii, p. 1118. *Census of Ireland 1891*, County Wicklow, Table vi, p. 1093. *Census of Ireland 1901*, County Wicklow, Table vii, p. 8.

31 Peter Haggett, *Geography: a modern synthesis*, (2nd ed. New York 1975) p. 473.

32 Population pyramids compiled from census data. *Census of Ireland 1881*, County Wicklow, Table xiii, p. 1152. *Census of Ireland 1891*, County Wicklow, Table xiii, p. 1127. *Census of Ireland 1901* County Wicklow, Table xv, p. 47.

33 Canon Donovan's Diary, undated, 1884.

34 *Thom's Official Directory of the United Kingdom of Great Britain and Ireland for the year 1881* (Dublin 1881) p. 1004.

35 *Thom's Directory* 1881, p. 35.

36 *Thom's Directory* 1881, p. 41.

37 *Thom's Directory* 1881, p. 1189.

38 *Thom's Directory* 1881, p. 1188.

39 *Slater's Directory* 1881, Towns of Leinster (London and Manchester 1881) p. 350.

40 *Leinster Leader*, 22 March 1890.

41 *Slater's Directory* 1881, p. 349.

42 *Leinster Leader*, 24 September 1898.

43 Fitzgerald, 'Dunlavin, Tornant and Tober', p. 222.

44 Fitzgerald, 'Dunlavin, Tornant and Tober', p. 224.

45 I am grateful to Mr. George Coleborn of Dunlavin Select Vestry for his help in this matter.

46 Dunlavin R. C. Parish Register, May 1818, (unpaginated).

47 *Slater's Directory* 1881, p. 351.

48 Army W.O. Form 1452, C. Ward, Paymaster's Office, Curragh Camp to Martin Kelly, 12 November 1872 and other documents in the possession of the author. I wish to place on record my thanks to the late Mr. Tommy Swaine of Dunlavin, who gave me these documents.

49 *Slater's Directory* 1881, p. 349.

50 Griffith, *Valuation*, pp 18–26.

51 See for example *Leinster Leader*, 28 July 1883; *Leinster Leader*, 5 July 1884; *Leinster Leader*, 2 August 1884; *Leinster Leader*, 25 August 1888; *Leinster Leader*, 25 October 1890.

52 P. H. Gulliver, 'Shopkeepers and farmers in south Kilkenny' in M. Silverman and P. H. Gulliver (eds) *Approaching the past*, (Columbia, 1992) p. 191.

53 N.U.I. Maynooth, Shearman papers, xvii, f. 168.

54 N.U.I. Maynooth, Shearman papers, xvii, f. 168.

55 N.U.I. Maynooth, *Calendar for Shearman papers*, p. 1.

56 N.U.I. Maynooth, Shearman papers, xvii, f. 168.

57 N.U.I. Maynooth, Shearman papers, xvii, f. 174.

58 *Leinster Leader*, 17 May 1890.

59 *Leinster Leader*, 15 March 1890.

60 John Bateman, *The great landowners of Great Britain and Ireland* (4th ed. 1883, Reprinted New York 1970) p. 462.

61 N.U.I. Maynooth, Shearman papers, xvii, f. 174.

62 *Slater's Directory* 1881, p. 351.

63 Canon Donovan's Diary, March 1888.

64 Bateman, *Landowners*, p. 452.

65 Chris Lawlor, 'Dunlavin – foundation, famine and beyond', p. 19.

66 Samuel Lewis, *A topographical dictionary of Ireland*, (2 vols, London 1837) i, p. 583.

67 William Nolan, 'Land and landscape in County Wicklow c. 1840' in Ken Hannigan and William Nolan (eds), *Wicklow, history and society*, (Dublin 1994) p. 689.

68 *Census of Ireland 1891*, County of Wicklow, Table viii, p. 1125.

69 Fitzgerald, 'Dunlavin, Tornant and Tober', p. 223.

70 *Slater's Directory* 1881, p. 350.

71 Canon Donovan's Diary, undated 1884.

72 Figures in this section taken from *Census of Ireland 1881*, County of Wicklow, Table xxx, p. 1161.

73 See for example E. P. O'Kelly's speech in *Leinster Leader*, 28 July 1883.

DONOVAN'S PARISH: RELIGION IN
DUNLAVIN, 1891–1901

1 Lord Walter Fitzgerald, 'Dunlavin, Tornant and Tober, County Wicklow' in *Journal of the Co. Kildare Archaeological Society*, vii, no. 4 (1913) p. 222. This plaque was intact when Fitzgerald was writing, but has since been destroyed and removed from the church.

2 N.U.I. Maynooth, Shearman papers, xvii, f. 168.

3 Chris Lawlor, 'Townland, ghosts and some reflections' in *Dunlavin – Donard – Davidstown Parish Link*, iv, no. 1, (1998) p. 3.

4 Samuel Lewis, *A topographical Dictionary, of Ireland*, (2 vols London 1837) i, p. 583.

5 *First Report of the Commissioners of Public Instruction, Ireland*, [C45], H. C. 1835, xxxiii, pp 104–105.

6 N.U.I. Maynooth, Shearman papers, xvii, f. 168.

7 Fr. Patrick Finn, 'Parish clergy down the years' in *Dunlavin – Donard – Davidstown Parish Link*, iii, no. 2, (1997) p. 2.

8 Dunlavin R. C. Parish Register, I, 1818 (unpaginated).

9 Dunlavin R. C. Parish Register, II, 1862 (unpaginated).

10 Dunlavin R. C. Parish Register, II, 1873, 1875, 1880 (unpaginated).

11 Canon Donovan's Diary, undated 1884. All other information given in this chapter is taken from Donovan's diary unless otherwise stated. The diary is unpaginated, but the month and the year are usually indicated and will appear in the text.

12 P. J. Hamell, *Maynooth students and ordinations index 1795–1895*, (Birr, 1982) pp 21, 57.

13 I am indebted to Mr. Gerry O'Neill of Blessington for this information.

14 *Irish Catholic Directory and Almanac 1897*, Clerical obituaries section, p. 329.

15 *Irish Catholic Directory and Almanac 1897*, Changes since going to press, flyleaf at beginning.

16 *Leinster Leader*, 14 September 1898.

17 *Leinster Leader*, 14 September 1898.

18 *Leinster Leader*, 14 September 1898.

19 I am indebted to Mr. David Sheehy, Dublin Diocesan Archives [D.D.A.], for this information.

20 *Addresses delivered on various occasions by Most Rev. Dr. Walsh Archbishop of Dublin*, (Dublin 1886) pp 174–175.
21 *Addresses by Dr. Walsh*, pp 184–185.
22 D.D.A., Walsh Papers, 1 November 1886, Byrne to [Walsh's secretary?], 402 / 3–5, Shelf 358.
23 I am indebted to Mr. David Sheehy for this information.
24 D.D.A., Walsh Papers, 3 August 1887, Brennan to Walsh, 402 / 6, 403 / 1–3, Shelf 359.
25 Emmet Larkin, 'The devotional revolution in Ireland 1850–75' in *American Historical Review*, lxxvii (1972).
26 For a discussion of this topic see Sean Connolly, *Religion and society in nineteenth century Ireland*, (Dundalk 1985) ch.3.
27 Dunlavin R. C. Parish Register, II, 1880 (unpaginated).
28 Lawrence J. Taylor, 'The language of belief' in M. Silverman and P. H. Gulliver (eds) *Approaching the past*, (Columbia 1992) p. 146.
29 Alice Taylor, *Quench the lamp*, (Dingle 1990) p. 51.
30 D.D.A. Walsh Papers, 1886, 402 / 3–5, Shelf 358.
31 Dunlavin R. C. Parish Register, iii, 29 March 1886 (unpaginated).
32 N.U.I. Maynooth, Shearman papers, vii, f. 51.
33 Finn, 'Parish clergy', p. 2.
34 Geraldine Lynch, 'The holy wells of County Wicklow: traditions and legends', in Ken Hannigan and William Nolan (eds), *Wicklow, history and society*, (Dublin 1994) p. 629.
35 Mary Norton, 'Dunlavin' in *Dunlavin Festival of Arts Brochure*, (1990) p. 9.
36 Chris Lawlor 'A pattern in time' in *Dunlavin Festival of Arts Brochure*, (1996) p. 52.
37 Fitzgerald, 'Dunlavin, Tornant and Tober', p. 230.
38 Samuel Russell McGee, *Dunlavin, Co. Wicklow – a retrospect* (Dublin 1935) p. 18.
39 McGee, *Retrospect*, p. 3.
40 McGee, *Retrospect*, pp 2, 3 and 17.
41 McGee, *Retrospect*, p. 8.
42 McGee, *Retrospect*, p. 5.
43 Address by Lord Plunkett, 20 August 1895. I am grateful to Mr. George Coleborn of Dunlavin Select Vestry for access to framed copies of this and other Church of Ireland addresses which are housed in Dunlavin.
44 McGee, *Retrospect*, p. 8.
45 *Irish Ecclesiastical Gazette*, 30 November 1894.
46 Representative Church Body Library, Dunlavin Select Vestry Minutes, 15 February 1871.
47 Address by Dr. Peacocke, 22 December 1899, (framed).
48 McGee, *Retrospect*, p. 8.
49 Rev. R. A. Warke, B.D., *St. Nicholas's Church and parish, Dunlavin* (1967) p. 13.
50 McGee, *Retrospect*, p. 11.
51 McGee, *Retrospect*, p. 13.
52 McGee, *Retrospect*, p. 11.
53 Warke, *St. Nicholas's Church*, p. 12.
54 *Irish Ecclesiastical Gazette*, 30 November 1894.
55 McGee, *Retrospect*, p. 4.
56 Address by Dr. Peacoke, 20 February 1901 (framed).
57 McGee, *Retrospect*, p. 14.
58 McGee, *Retrospect*, p. 19.
59 McGee, *Retrospect*, pp 8–9.

DONOVAN'S POLITICS: NATIONALIST
DUNLAVIN, 1881–1901

1 N.U.I. Maynooth, Shearman papers, xvii, f. 168.
2 N.U.I. Maynooth, Shearman papers, xvii, f. 168.
3 *Report of the Commission of Inquiry into the state of the law and practice in respect of the occupation of land in Ireland II* (hereafter *Devon Commission*)' [C616] H.C. 1845, xxi, p. 562.
4 *Devon Commission*, p. 562.
5 *Devon Commission*, p. 562.
6 *Devon Commission*, p. 562.
7 *Devon Commission*, p. 563.
8 *Devon Commission*, p. 563.
9 N.U.I. Maynooth, Shearman papers, xvii, f. 168.
10 N.U.I. Maynooth, Shearman papers, xvii, f. 168.
11 *Slater's Directory 1881* (Leinster), p. 350. See also Griffith, *Valuation*, p. 26.
12 *Leinster Leader*, 4 June 1898.
13 *Leinster Leader*, 26 July 1890.
14 *Leinster Leader*, 4 June 1898.
15 *The Nation*, 25 October 1879.
16 Michael Davitt, *The fall of feudalism in Ireland* (London 1904) p. 213.
17 National Library of Ireland, Ms. 842, November 1880.
18 Roy Foster, 'Parnell and his neighbours' in Ken Hannigan and William Nolan (eds), *Wicklow, history and society*, (Dublin 1994) p. 904.
19 *Report of Her Majesty's commissioners of inquiry into the working of the Landlord and Tenant (Ireland) Act 1870, and the acts amending the same* (hereinafter called the *Bessborough Commission*), [C2779], H. C. 1881, xix, pp 36–42, 50–57 and 132–136.
20 *Bessborough Commission*, p. 134.
21 *Bessborough Commission*, pp 132–133, 51–53 and 36–37.
22 *Bessborough Commission*, p. 38.
23 *Bessborough Commission*, pp 55–56 and 134.
24 National Archives, Arrest Books, Protection of Persons and Property Act, October 1881.
25 *Leinster Leader*, 14 April 1883.
26 *Freeman's Journal*, 18 October 1882.
27 I am indebted to Dr. Terry Dooley for this information.
28 See for example *Leinster Leader*, 28 July 1883; *Leinster Leader*, 5 July 1884; *Leinster Leader*, 2 August 1884; *Leinster Leader*, 25 August 1888; *Leinster Leader*, 25 October 1890.
29 *The handbook of the Drogheda chemical manure company 1897*, p. 73.
30 Griffith, *Valuation* pp 10–38.
31 See footnote 72, first chapter.
32 Cora Crampton 'The Tullow line' in *Journal of the West Wicklow Historical Society*, i (1983–1984) p. 8.
33 All information regarding the meeting on 22 July 1883 is taken from *Leinster Leader*, 28 July 1883.
34 Canon Donovan's Diary, undated, 1884. As in chapter 2, all other information given in this chapter is taken from Donovan's diary unless otherwise stated.

35 Griffith, *Valuation*, pp 25–26.
36 *Leinster Leader*, 5 July 1884.
37 *Leinster Leader*, 2 August 1884. It is possible that the *Leader* exaggerated the numbers attending the meeting, but it was obviously a large affair and very successful.
38 *Leinster Leader*, 5 July 1884.
39 *Leinster Leader*, 28 July 1883. W. J. Corbet of Spring Farm, Delgany, was nominated for Wicklow at Parnell's insistence in 1880, served as M.P. for Wicklow from 1880–1885 and for Wicklow East from 1885–1892. Defeated as a Parnellite in 1892, he was elected in 1895, ending his parliamentary career in 1900. (See Hannigan and Nolan (eds) *Wicklow, history and society,* footnote p. 720).
40 Despite the election of Byrne and Corbet, life remained hard for the labourers until well into the 20th century. (See – Ross M. Connolly, 'A rightful place in the sun – the struggle of the farm and rural labourers of County Wicklow' in Hannigan and Nolan (eds) *Wicklow, history and society,* pp 911–925.
41 Even in July 1887, when the Peter's pence 'assumed larger than ordinary dimensions' due to Pope Leo XIII's golden jubilee, only £31 0s. 6d. was collected.
42 *Leinster Leader*, 28 July 1888.
43 *Leinster Leader*, 11 August 1888.
44 'Hurley' could be a reference to a hurley stick. For the existence of an Orange lodge in Donard, see Ruan O'Donnell, 'The rebellion of 1798 in County Wicklow' in Hannigan and Nolan (eds) *Wicklow, history and society,* p. 369 [1799], N.U.I. Maynooth, Shearman papers, xvii, f. 167 [1835] and f. 170v. [1862]. Again the attendance figures could be slightly exaggerated by the Leader.
45 *Leinster Leader*, 1 February 1890.
46 *Leinster Leader*, 8 February 1890.
47 *Leinster Leader*, 31 May 1890.
48 *Leinster Leader*, 26 July 1890.
49 The Land League and National League papers in the National Library of Ireland do not include the records of the Dunlavin branch, so the local historian of Dunlavin is dependant on passing mentions of Dunlavin in other documents such as Ms. 842, Minutes of Rathvilly branch.

50 *Leinster Leader*, 28 July 1883.
51 James Whittle, *Sons of St. Nicholas – a history of Dunlavin GAA club* (Dunlavin 1984) p. 4.
52 N.U.I. Maynooth, Shearman papers, xvii, f. 167.
53 Family Records, Chris Lawlor was the author's great grandfather.
54 Whittle, *Sons of St. Nicholas*, p. 4.
55 Whittle, *Sons of St. Nicholas*, p. 5.
56 *Leinster Leader*, 15 April 1890.
57 *Leinster Leader*, 8 November 1890; *Leinster Leader*, 15 November 1890; *Leinster Leader*, 22 November 1890. See also Whittle, *Sons of St. Nicholas*, pp 6–7.
58 *Leinster Leader*, 12 April 1890.
59 Whittle, *Sons of St. Nicholas*, p. 8.
60 *Leinster Leader*, 25 October 1890.
61 *Leinster Leader*, 27 December 1890.
62 Whittle, *Sons of St. Nicholas*, p. 8.
63 F.S.L. Lyons, *Ireland since the famine*, (4th ed., London, 1976) p. 261.
64 *Leinster Leader*, 31 October 1893.
65 *The handbook of the Drogheda chemical manure company 1897*, pp. 73.
66 *Freeman's Journal*, 20 May 1894.
67 Fr. Frederick A. Donovan was elevated to the status of canon on 10 January 1893. It is interesting to note that the address presented to Donovan on 12 March 1893 does not bear the names of any leading Parnellite families in the parish. (See Chris Lawlor, The Wicklow world of Canon F. A. Donovan: Dunlavin 1884–1896, unpublished MA thesis, N.U.I. Maynooth), Appendix 8.
68 *Leinster Leader*, 17 May 1890. The reference is to the acquittal of a protestant rate-collector by Dunlavin petty sessions in the face of all the evidence. The collector, John Barrett had obviously embezzled over £120 before declaring himself to be bankrupt.
69 R. F. Foster, *Modern Ireland 1600–1972*, (London, 1988), p. 427.
70 *Leinster Leader*, 4 June 1898.
71 Samuel Russell McGee, *Dunlavin – a retrospect* (Dublin, 1935), p. 2.
72 J. C. Beckett, *The making of modern Ireland 1603–1923* (5th ed., London, 1973) p. 415.